FORD
CONSUL/ZEPHYR SIX/ZEPHYR ZODIAC MK1

Michael Allen

CONTENTS

Foulis

Haynes

A FOULIS Motoring Book

First published 1986

© **Haynes Publishing Group**

Published by:
Haynes Publishing Group,
Sparkford, Near Yeovil,
Somerset BA22 7JJ

Haynes Publications Inc.
861 Lawrence Drive, Newbury
Park, California 91320, USA

**British Library Cataloguing in
Publication Data**

Allen, Michael,
    Ford Consul/Zephyr Six/Zephyr Zodiac
super profile.-(Super profile)
    1.   Consul automobile–History
    2.   Zephyr automobile–History
    3.   Zodiac automobile–History
    I. Title   II.   Series
    629.2'222   TL215.F7

    ISBN 0-85429-497-X

**Library of Congress catalog
card number**

    86-80519

Editor: Rod Grainger
Page layout: Peter Kay
Series photographer: Andrew
Morland
Road tests: Courtesy of *Autocar*
and *Motor*
Printed in England, by:
J.H. Haynes & Co. Ltd

Further titles in this series will be published at regular
intervals. For information on new titles please contact
your bookseller or write to the publisher.

FOREWORD

"The Ford Motor Co. have already two historic innovations to their credit; the T model, introduced in 1908, was the first car which could be owned, driven and maintained by unskilled persons driving over any road conditions in any part of the world; the introduction of the V8 power unit in 1932 marked the first occasion on which a car having a power/weight ratio of some 70hp/ton and a maximum speed of circa 80mph was built in very large quantities and offered to the US public at the exceedingly modest price of £125 at the then current exchange rate. Thus, the Ford Co. were the first to give motoring to the masses and the first to give performance to the many.

The new Zephyr which emanates from the British section of the Ford group of companies is yet another first, for it allies the high performance and (by modern standards) modest price characteristic of the V8, with a general roadworthiness and stability which virtually take it out of the family motoring class and put it into the sports-car category in a manner obviously remote from the original intention of the designers."

So said *The Motor* in October 1951 when publishing their eagerly awaited road test report of the new Zephyr Six. Comments such as these had in fact been anticipated, for much praise had already been heaped upon the Consul by the motoring press as the four-cylinder model had been the first to enter production, and an early example had become available as a press demonstrator earlier in the year. Now there was no doubt, Dagenham had produced a brace of cars which were truly outstanding amongst their type, and which, while innovative in several important respects, were nevertheless being offered at prices which were recognised immediately as representing the best value yet from a company whose products were already noted above all else for their sheer value-for-money appeal.

As a schoolboy interested in most things mechanical, I was attracted to these smooth-looking cars from their early days, although, as my father never owned a Mk1, it was to be some years before I had a really close association with the model. In more recent years, the past dozen in fact, using six-cylinder Mk1s as everyday transport, and being actively involved with the owners' club has resulted in a strong personal association with the Mk1s which I fully intend to be a permanent one.

It has been a particular pleasure therefore to write this Super Profile, and there are many people who deserve thanks for a variety of assistance willingly given: Matthew Carter, of *Autocar,*

and John Thorpe, of *Motor,* for their permission to reproduce contemporary road test reports from their respective magazines; Andy Tutt and Steve Scott for their participation in producing "Owner's View"; the Ford Motor Company in the persons of David Burgess-Wise, Steve Clark, and Sheila Knapman, for the engine number lists appearing in "Evolution", and the archive photographs used to illustrate certain examples of the model.

Preserved and restored Mk1s are featured in the other illustrations, and my thanks for photographing these go to Andrew Morland, whilst for their help in making the cars available my gratitude is owed to the following: Neil Tee, John Walker, Simon Long, John Mawby, Mick Johnson, Tom Bowles, Ray Greenaway, Rowland Oliver, Dave McNiece, Robin Weathersbee, Don Stangroom, Mike Hine, and Dave Cropper, the last named who also at very short notice spent much time preparing the site in his orchard where the cars were photographed. Finally, my thanks to Keith Trotter for photographing export Mk1s on his recent travels, and Howard Foottit for the loan of old motoring literature.

Michael Allen

Zephyr

Zodiac

HISTORY

Family tree

By the time it came to the end of its 19 year production run, Henry Ford's legendary Model T was so thoroughly outdated that Ford himself felt entirely justified in christening the replacement car the Model A; so signifying the beginning of a new era in Ford automobiles.

Advanced almost out of recognition by comparison with its predecessor, the Model A quickly set about restoring the company's fortunes which had flagged considerably during the final years of the ageing Model T. The new car was greeted with genuine enthusiasm everywhere, except, that is, in Britain, where even the availability of a derivative with a small-bore engine to beat the horse power tax failed to result in anything like sufficient sales, as smaller home-grown competition much more appropriate to the British market was gaining ground. This situation in Britain was all the more serious as Ford's magnificent new purpose-built plant by the side of the river Thames at Dagenham was due to commence operation late in 1931 when production would be transferred from the company's Trafford Park, Manchester works.

It was as a result of these considerations that the 8hp Model Y Ford entered production at Dagenham in August 1932. Although designed in America, this was the first Ford created for a specific market outside the United States. Meeting with instant success, and becoming the first Ford Popular in 1935, the Y type was joined in 1934 by the 10hp Model C, before restyled and improved 8 and 10hp models followed in 1937 from which evolved the first of the Anglia and Prefect models. The Model Y had indeed been a lifesaver for Ford of Britain, and it was with these and the subsequent small Fords that Dagenham established itself as one of the major motor manufacturing centres in Britain in the 1930s. This small-car range was of course also the company's mainstay in the immediate postwar years, before eventually evolving into the "upright" Popular of the 1950s after Dagenham had launched its modern 100E Anglia/Prefect range.

Meanwhile however, there had been another range of Dagenham built Fords produced in much smaller numbers. In March 1932, Henry Ford had unveiled what was to be the last of his engineering miracles — the one-piece-block V8 engine. At a stroke, old Henry had added high-performance to the many other virtues of the products bearing his name; and this 30hp rated 3.6-litre unit, later bored out to 3.9-litres, was destined to be the principle American Ford powerplant for more than 20 years. At first, a few V8 models were imported into Britain, with Dagenham eventually going into limited production of this type in 1935 in order to satisfy the small demand here for this class of car. Both 30hp and 22hp-rated models were produced for the British market, with the latter being powered by the narrow-bored version of the V8 engine reducing its capacity to 2.2-litres. Like the 8

and 10hp cars, these much larger models featured separate chassis and body construction, Model T inspired non-independent transverse leaf spring suspension at both front and rear, mechanically operated brakes and clutch, three-speed gearboxes, sidevalve engines, and a 6 volt electrical system.

The final variation of the V8 theme in Britain came late in 1947, at which time Dagenham announced the V8 Pilot that was to complete the early postwar range which since the resumption of production in 1945 had consisted of just the E04A Anglia and E93A Prefect cars. Although bearing a marked similarity in appearance, by comparison with its predecessors the Pilot was quite lavishly equipped; with cloth upholstery, a heater, rear centre armrests, door armrests and silk doorpulls all combining to give an inviting interior, whilst comprehensive instrumentation, a horn ring, and an extremely accurate column-mounted gearchange lever would please the driver. Refinements such as an anti-roll bar, and Girling "Hydro Mech" brakes were incorporated into the traditional Ford running gear, giving worthwhile improvements in the general roadworthiness which now more closely matched the standards of performance provided by the legendary 30hp V8 engine; although roadholding and handling did still fall short of what was being achieved elsewhere with more modern designs.

Large, and fully equipped, the Pilot was quite an expensive car, although in typical Ford fashion, it was still offering a combination of performance, accomodation, equipment, and overall quality which could not be matched at the price. That it was excellent value in fact was never in doubt; but, weighing in at 30cwt, and offering but 16/17mpg fuel economy at a time of strict steel quotas and continued petrol rationing, the Pilot was a somewhat extravagant car. Nor could it conceal its 1930s ancestry, and in fact was intended only as an interim top-of-the-range car to be produced in limited numbers by comparison with its smaller stablemates (which used much less of the steel quota per car) during the time it would take to develop a completely new medium/large car.

Concept and design

In addition to producing a new model which would offer the performance and accommodation of the Pilot, with new found handling qualities and much better overall economy for this type of car, it was just as important now to produce a medium-powered version with which to fill the noticeable gap in the Ford range above the 10hp Prefect. Consultations with the parent company resulted in Dagenham receiving the go-ahead to design an advanced new model which whilst being styled on broadly similar lines to the new, and much larger American Ford scheduled for release in the summer of 1948, would otherwise differ almost totally from anything previously bearing the Ford name.

By comparison with the then more traditional separate chassis and body combination, all-steel monocoque construction offered useful weight savings with actual improvements in rigidity being possible. Bearing this in mind, and the fact that an as yet untried but obviously quite brilliant front suspension system designed specifically for use with a monocoque body was available to them, an integrally constructed body-cum-chassis unit was chosen by the Dagenham team. The new suspension system, named after the American Ford

engineer credited with its design, the "MacPherson strut" transferred its loads directly into the bodyshell's strong scuttle/bulkhead region from upper mounting points in the inner wing, so obviating the need for the separate load-bearing subframe demanded by the conventional double wishbone independent front end arrangements. A weight saving was gained without additional effort in that direction, therefore the need to pursue weight saving for its own sake in the structure itself was reduced. All of these considerations resulted in an extremely rigid four-door bodyshell of great structural strength to which was added unstressed bolt-on outer panels comprising the front grille housing, front wings, and lower-half rear wings.

Developed in conjunction with Briggs Motor Bodies, Ford's traditional suppliers who themselves had occupied premises at Dagenham since 1932, the new body featured greater internal width in combination with the same headroom as the Pilot, but within usefully more compact external dimensions. Rear compartment kneeroom was reduced slightly, as the seat here was brought forward appreciably ahead of the rear axle line in the interests of improved riding comfort by comparison with the previous car.

Mention has already been made of the strut type front suspension units, the upper mounting point of which consisted of a composite steel/rubber block housing bolted to the inner wing. This mounting block featured a built in heavy duty bearing in which the strut centre spindle rotated, acting therefore as an extremely long king pin. Its upper half embraced by a coil spring, the strut was also the hydraulic shock absorber, and was located at the bottom by a track control arm and a forward

mounted anti-roll bar. Operating in conjunction with this system was a Burman worm and peg steering box and a three piece track rod arrangement. Longitudinally mounted semi-elliptic leaf springs at the rear completed the departure from the traditional set up of the previous models, whilst an all hydraulic braking system was another notable advance.

Few government decisions can have been more timely to a British motor manufacturer than the one in 1947, to abandon the horsepower tax, was to the Ford Motor Company. The previous necessity to produce engines with bore diameters determined by nothing other then the need to be within a horsepower rating was now removed, conveniently allowing Dagenham to be the first to take full advantage of the new situation. Wider bores would allow a shorter stroke and lower piston speeds, therefore higher rpm. Also because of its reduced throws a more rigid crankshaft was possible. Additionally, larger bores allow much larger valves to be fitted and correspondingly better breathing than is the case with a narrow-bore ohv engine. Now more power from a given capacity with higher, but safer engine operating speeds were obtainable without tax penalties.

In view of the performance and economy required from the new car, engine sizes of around 1.5 and rather more than 2-litres were desirable, and this was to be achieved by producing in-line four- and six-cylinder units sharing common bore centres and bore and stroke measurements. This enabled all the moving parts other than the camshaft and crankshaft, but including the bearings in which they ran, to be common to both engine types. A hydraulic clutch was another new Ford feature but, whilst also being a new design, the gearbox followed established Ford practice in the provision of only three forward gears of which first was without synchromesh. The gearbox was common to both engine types, as was an open propeller shaft to a new hypoid axle which differed slightly in ratio between the four- and six-cylinder models, the larger engine pulling the higher gear.

The sharing of many components – including almost the entire running gear, and all body panels from the windscreen rearwards – allowed the production of two models which despite their obvious similarities were nevertheless two quite distinct cars in respect of performance, and frontal appearance too. The latter being due to the six-cylinder engine requiring a longer engine compartment which was desirable in itself as a visual hint of the more powerful engine under the bonnet.

At a time when exporting was of such prime importance that a car manufacturer's steel quota actually depended upon the company's export performance, the choice of "Consul" as the name for the new four-cylinder car was apt indeed, and it was with this title that the car appeared at the Earls Court Motor Show in October 1950. Alongside it of course was the six-cylinder car which was re-introducing the name "Zephyr". This name had formerly graced the parent company's Lincoln Division's low-priced V12-engined model; that car having been recently deleted as part of an overall policy in which Lincoln would concentrate on their luxury Continental and Cosmopolitan. The full name "Zephyr Six" on the new English Ford would avoid confusion with the former V12 powered American car. Billed as the "Five Star Cars", with "oversquare" engines, "centre slung" within the wheelbase seating, MacPherson strut suspension, all-round hydraulic brakes, and the monocoque construction being regarded as the

five "Star" features, these revolutionary Fords were recognised immediately as trend-setters even before the public or the press were able to sample them on the road.

Production

Inheriting only a handful or so of parts used in previous Dagenham products, these new cars necessitated considerable sums spent on new machine-tools etc., including the introduction of process-through, or transfer-line machinery on which the new cylinder blocks could be produced at approximately twice the rate possible with previous methods. Completely new crankshaft grinding machinery, gear cutting, splining, and multi-drilling machinery etc., was installed. Additionally, throughout the development period, considerable thought was given to ease of production, including the final assembly techniques which, for example, eliminated pit work; therefore easing the task of assembly-line workers and so enabling them to maintain high workmanship standards at increased production rates. Prototype testing was not completed at the time the cars were exhibited at Earls Court, and it was not in fact until New Year's Day 1951 that production got under way.

Consuls were the first to leave the assembly lines, going into mass production almost immediately as the company pursued its policy of first satisfying the demand for the more economical models in its range; only limited production of

C O N S U L

six-cylinder cars being scheduled for 1951. This resulted in considerable frustration amongst would-be Zephyr buyers, particularly so towards the end of the year when famous competition driver Raymond Mays, and renowned technical journalist Laurence Pomeroy junior, both wrote in the motoring press glowing reports of the Zephyr's combination of performance and handling qualities. Nevertheless, despite long waiting lists for this model, it was not until well into 1952 that production was stepped up, and even then to a level still somewhat below that of the Consul. By this time, the new Fords could be seen in numbers on a world-wide basis, as well over half the production was playing its part in earning foreign currency for Britain, being shipped overseas in both built-up and completely knocked-down form for local assembly in areas such as Australia, New Zealand, Singapore, and India where Ford had assembly facilities. The specifications only varied very slightly on the export cars according to local conditions, with the absence of heaters and the provision of a four-bladed engine cooling fan for hot climates, for instance. Local assembly did result in different paint and trim colours being available in some territories.

As matters improved at home, with the effects of wartime really beginning to fade, expansion was possible, and the Consul/Zephyr range expanded considerably during 1953 with first the convertibles, and then the addition of the luxurious Zephyr Zodiac. Slight trim changes both inside and out on the Consul and Zephyr Six accompanied the introduction of the Zodiac, and three years since its introduction the range seemed more competitive than ever, with constantly rising production still being unable to meet the demand.

The two-door convertible models had been developed for

Ford by Carbodies of Coventry, a specialist concern which built drophead models for several manufacturers. In the case of these Ford cars, carbodies built up the cars on standard floorpans supplied by Dagenham but then braced them to restore the rigidity lost by the absence of the steel roof. The next variation on the basic theme came late in 1954, and was even more of an "outside" job, being the estate car conversion which coachbuilders E.D. Abbott had developed entirely independently, but which nevertheless got the approval of the Ford Motor Company. However, whereas the convertible cars were listed by Ford alongside the saloons, the estate cars never were, with the customer having to arrange the conversion through the dealer who in turn could arrange for the new car to be delivered straight to Abbotts from Dagenham. A better alternative in fact was to take delivery of the car and then arrange the conversion work independently, as this avoided paying purchase tax on the conversion which was in effect now being carried out on a used car.

Continued improvement in production facilities saw many more Zephyrs take to the road in 1954, and for those wishing for something quicker still there were a variety of tuning kits available from specialists, featuring such as re-worked high compression cylinder heads, triple carburettor installations, and six branch exhaust manifolds. Consuls, too, could be treated in similar fashion, with inexpensive twin carburettor systems, or just a four branch exhaust manifold which would give a useful increase in acceleration.

In August 1955 the Borg Warner semi-automatic overdrive became available as optional equipment on the six-cylinder models only. Two months later, the range made its last Earls Court appearance, before being replaced in February 1956 by the larger, Mk2 Consul Zephyr and Zodiac.

Reasons for discontinuation

After the introduction of the Zephyr Zodiac, the range was complete in so far as Ford were concerned. Carbodies could meet the small demand for convertibles, and there were no plans for additional variations to be built at Dagenham as this would only disrupt production of the saloons with which, despite continued improvement in production facilities, it was unlikely that the demand could be met for some years. This simply meant that any face-lifting exercise or change in basic mechanical specification would have been wasting some of the profits being made out of this range. A far better plan was to start now on development work of an eventual, Mk2 replacement model which could be brought to the ready for production stage in time to take over when interest began to wane in the existing models.

Whether the Mk1 range had peaked at the time of its replacement in February 1956 is a little difficult to judge. Production in 1955, its last, and best year, was about 7% greater than the previous year, a remarkable achievement indeed for a five year old model which had changed so little since its introduction, and was the oldest model in its class. In January 1956 however, it was joined in production by the Mk2 range, and was soon being run down as stocks of the new model were built up prior to the February launch. Production rates for the Mk2 were naturally slower at first before familiarity with the model was gained, and then a strike in the industry outside Ford nevertheless adversely affected Dagenham production, and this was followed by the Suez crisis. These last two factors would of course have had similar adverse effects on Mk1 production, so spoiling any chance of it building further on its previous year, and as it would have been into its 7th year by the time these problems passed it seems very unlikely that it could have enjoyed any further real success. As it was, after mid 1957 the Mk2 models quickly overtook the Mk1's 1955 figures, going on to dominate the market for this class of car beyond the end of the decade.

Motorsport

It fell to the Consul to score the model's first major success when, in April 1952, Ken Wharton drove to outright victory in the Dutch International Tulip Rally, after giving an impressive display of the Consul's versatility in a variety of special tests during the event. These included timed hill climbs and, right at the end, a 10 lap race around the grand prix circuit at Zandvoort. Nothing less than a win in the race for cars in the up-to-1600cc class would do if Ken Wharton was to win the rally, and in fact he pushed the Consul hard enough round Zandvoort to lap the tailenders at the finish.

Although never repeating this outright victory, Consuls, as both private and, occasionally, works entries, did compete from time to time in the major international events. A class win and second place were recorded in the 1954 Tulip Rally, where the Consul's principle opposition came from the Jowett Javelins. Although not highly placed, Consuls were amongst the finishers in what was an extremely tough 1955 Monte Carlo Rally. The Consul was never seriously developed as a competition car however for no other reason than the Zephyr Six, with its far greater performance, had much more potential as both a standard production, or modified touring car in the tough international events.

In fact, it was almost wholly the Zephyr's obvious potential that resulted in Ford setting up a competition department late in 1952 in readiness for a serious attempt at the forthcoming Monte Carlo Rally in January 1953. Four Zephyrs were entered in the over 1500cc unlimited class. In the event, the result depended entirely on the final 47 mile long mountain circuit stage, with the works Zephyr of Maurice Gatsonides emerging as the winner after having completed the circuit within two seconds of the target time for the over 1500cc cars, and being variously reported as just one, or two seconds faster than Ian Appleyard's MkVII Jaguar. This was all the more creditable as all cars were running as standard models in respect of their mechanical specification, the only modifications being the addition of navigational and timekeeping aids etc.. In fact, the works Zephyrs were even running on remould tyres, a situation brought about as there were no suitable 13 inch snow tyres available, and apparently no major tyre manufacturer was interested in supplying Ford with covers for the event. This resulted in an approach to Tyresoles, the Wembley-based retreading experts, who successfully remoulded some 13 inch covers with a very bold pattern tread. That the 2.3 litre Ford had beaten the 3.4-litre engined Jaguar in a straight fight in the mountains (both were in the unlimited capacity class) was largely due to the more compact Zephyr's superior handling around numerous hairpin bends, and Gatsonides' unique brake-cooling methods which, quite literally, involved helpers at strategic points ready to throw bucketfuls of cold water over the Zephyr's front brakes as it passed!

Other successes in 1953 were

an outright win in the Norwegian Viking Rally by a locally entered Zephyr, whilst later in the year Nancy Mitchell won the Ladies Cup on the Lisbon Rally at the wheel of a works car. A high compression cylinder head and triple SU carburettors put the Zephyrs into the Modified Touring Car category, and it was in this configuration that the works-entered cars contested the 1954 "Monte". The additional handicaps imposed on the modified cars however proved too difficult to overcome, and although both T.C. "Cuth" Harrison, and Gatsonides put up an excellent showing on the timed climb of the Col de Leques, which was one of the principal special tests, the Zephyrs were out of the top placings this time, with Cuth Harrison being best in 13th place overall.

In March 1954, success came in the RAC Rally in Britain, when Cuth and Edward Harrison drove their Zephyr to victory in the saloon car category, actually finishing 3rd overall on the rally behind two Triumph TR2s. This was the same Zephyr the pair had used on the recent "Monte", but like the other works cars it was now back to a standard engine specification, a set up which was retained by the works Zephyrs for the Tulip Rally a month later; an event in which, at the end, everything rested on the result of the Zandvoort race in the up-to-2600cc class. Either Sheila Van Damm (Sunbeam), or Denis Scott (Zephyr) could win this class by winning the race, and it was the Sunbeam which broke clear from the grid. Unperturbed, however, Scott settled in behind

Zephyr Six

before finally nosing the Zephyr ahead on the last lap to prove that it was just as much at home on a racing circuit as it was over the mountain passes. Another outright victory looked certain in August, with Dutchman Maurice Gatsonides in the lead in the Weisbaden Rally with just about 150 kilometres to the finish. Then, a truck coming out of a side turning left the "Flying Dutchman" with nowhere to go. Fortunately, apart from a piece of triplex screen embedded in his hand, "Gatso" was unhurt: but the tragedy was that the Zephyr was good old VHK 194 in which he had won the "Monte" the previous year – and it was wrecked.

Many private entrants, too, favoured the Zephyr for competition work, and on occasions met with real success in the major events. After a tough journey across Europe to Monte Carlo in 1955 the best placed Zephyr (10th) was the perfectly standard car owned and entered by Gerry Burgess. Still to come was the mountain circuit and a five lap speed test around Monaco before the final results would be known. A spectacular mountain drive saw Burgess move up to 4th place overall, although at the expense of the car somewhat in that it had now "lost" top gear. Nevertheless, five laps at full-bore in second gear around Monaco were just sufficient for Burgess to hang on to his position, and so collect the trophy awarded to the highest placed British car/driver combination. Another Zephyr victory, which many regard as its finest, also took place in 1955 in the hands of a private entrant. This was Vic Preston's excellent drive to outright victory in the East African Safari, when only 20 out of the 57 starters managed to finish the 2,500 mile event staged largely over unmade roads. The Ladies Cup went to Zephyr entrant Mary Wright, her car being one of the two other Zephyrs amongst the surviving 20 cars.

Meanwhile, the works cars were still going strong, with Cuth Harrison adding two more class wins to the Zephyr's total in 1955. These being on the RAC Rally, and the Tulip. These excellent results were of course achieved long before the big-money days, and the "homologation specials" of recent years which unfortunately don't really have much in common with the showroom article, therefore not giving the present-day owner much idea of the capabilities of his ordinary car. Whereas, a sticker in the windscreen of Walter Mitty's Mk1 Zephyr (complete with remoulds!) proudly proclaiming the "Monte" victory, would appear to have been valid enough.

Review of model's success

From the Ford Motor Company's point of view this was an extremely successful range. The Consul quickly established itself as the leading contender in the increasingly popular 1.5-litre class which was a whole new market for Ford, and continued to hold its own comfortably right to the end, despite the regular appearance of newer opposition in this important sector. As a competition car, the Zephyr brought the company much esteem, its exploits not only proving this model's remarkably versatile performance, but more importantly underlining the rugged qualities which all of Ford's products possessed, and the Zephyr's results undoubtedly helped to sell more than half the total production of this range as a whole to overseas customers at a time when exporting was vital to Britain's economy.

Finally, there is the success of the basic concept and design. A smooth "three box" bodyshell housing an oversquare engine, MacPherson struts, and hydraulic reservoirs situated high upon the bulkhead from where they were operated by pendant pedals, was unique in 1951. Yet, 15 years or so later, this layout had been so widely copied as to be thought of as boringly conventional by much of the motoring press. Whether it was boring is purely a matter of opinion but that it had become conventional is a fact which makes this range one of the most significant postwar British cars.

Zephyr Zodiac

EVOLUTION

Evolution

The chassis and engine numbers were the same when the cars were new. This number is prefixed by the model designation code, and appears on the chassis plate mounted on the left-hand-side of the front panel and is additionally stamped into the front suspension upper mounting point on the right-hand-side of the car. The engine number is stamped into the horizontal flat surface on the cylinder block adjacent to the right-hand-side engine mounting bracket.

Model designation code

E = England /, 0 = 1950 (model announcement year) /, T = 4 cyl' OHV /, TT = 6 cyl' OHV /, A = Passenger car /, L = Left-hand-drive.

Examples

EOTAL: Left-hand-drive Consul.
EOTTA: Right-hand-drive Zephyr Six or Zephyr Zodiac.

Major change points

October 1950: Introduced at the Earls Court Motor Show as the Consul (4 cyl) four-door saloon at £532, and the Zephyr Six four-door saloon at £608. A heater and demisting unit, leather upholstery, and push-button radio available at extra cost.

January 1st 1951: First production Consul assembled at Dagenham.

February 12th 1951: First production Zephyr Six assembled at Dagenham.

March 1951: Front struts interchangeable from side-to-side introduced. Original struts had "handed" steering connections.

April 1951: Purchase tax increase raised the prices to £662 for the Consul and £759 for the Zephyr Six.

June 1951: Retracting spring incorporated in handbrake system, connected between the equaliser lever and gearbox support member (from engine no. EOTA 9232, and EOTTA 0800). Gasket introduced between top of suspension strut and inner-wing mounting point.

July 1951: Wider exhaust manifold clamps. Smaller hot-spot on Zephyr Six inlet manifold. New choke control, now lockable in any position by rotating the choke knob.

August 1951: Exhaust tailpipes increased in length by 1.5 inches. Machined face introduced on rear axle drive-shaft flange to improve propeller shaft alignment.

October 1951: Manufacturer's price increases announced with the Consul now at £717, and the Zephyr Six £816. Redesigned facia shown on cars displayed at Earls Court Motor Show, but not yet incorporated in production models. Prototype of the projected Zephyr Six convertible also displayed.

December 1951: Modified front suspension units introduced with metal piston-rod shroud assembly instead of the original rubber gaiter. Rocker cover gasket thickness increased from $1/8$in to $3/16$in.

January 1952: Improved gearbox extension oil seal.

February 1952: New axle ratios: Consul 4.556:1 (4.625:1 previously), Zephyr Six 4.444:1 (4.375:1 previously). Notification of this change is in Ford Service Letter No. 2 1952 series, dated 25/2/52. No engine numbers relating to this change are given, and the owners handbook records this change as occurring in November 1952 when revised 1st and 2nd gear ratios were introduced. With the assembly removed, the ratios can be identified by the figures stamped on the crownwheel: 8/37 = 4.625:1, 9/41 = 4.556:1 (Consuls); 8/35 = 4.375:1, 9/40 = 4.444:1 (Zephyr Sixes). Appropriately modified speedometer gears were introduced simultaneously.

June 1952: Reshaped fuel filler pipe adopted to lessen blowback when filling up.

September 1952: New dashboard and instrument housing as shown at Earls Court in 1951 now incorporated in production. Double acting vacuum pump replaced earlier single acting type for improved windscreen wiper efficiency. Battery heatshield introduced.

November 1952: Lower first and second gear ratios introduced from engine numbers EOTA 67119, and EOTTA 22717.

December 1952: Pendant "spoon" type accelerator pedal introduced.

February 1953: Modified dipstick with shorter dipstick tube from engine numbers EOTA 78591 and EOTTA 32790.

March 1953: Strengthened baffles to improve silencer life.

April 1953: Improved clutch drive plates with 6 torsion springs in place of the previous 4 (Consul), and 5 (Zephyr Six). Redesigned engine/gearbox mountings in which block type insulators replaced the circular type, and were not retrospectively interchangeable due to slight differences now in the front cross tube, and a new gearbox extension housing. Original first and second gear ratios re-adopted from engine numbers EOTA 86496 and EOTTA 39096. Purchase tax reductions now gave prices of £666 and £754.

May 1953: Steering box modified with increased diameter worm and new ball peg.

August 1953: Heavy grade (grade 3) coil springs fitted on Zephyr Six only, with grade 2 springs on Consul only and grade 1 springs deleted. Previously any of the three spring grades were fitted in pairs to either Consuls or Zephyrs according to the supply position.

October 1953: Zephyr Zodiac introduced at £851, differing from the Zephyr Six in the following respects. Externally: two tone paintwork, chrome wheeltrim rings, whitewall tyres, gold plated name scripts, wing mirrors, spot lamp, fog lamp, reversing lamp, rear reflectors, lockable fuel filler cap. Interior: two tone doortrims with lower section carpeted to match floor carpet, two tone leather upholstery, woollen headlining, larger rubber heel pad in driving compartment, cigar lighter, electric clock, vanity mirror on passenger's sunvisor. Additional equipment and specification differences: windscreen washers, high compression cylinder head (7.5:1), chrome plated top piston rings, heavy duty battery, rubber insulators for rear spring mounting with rear axle, heater and demister.

Changes to the entire range in October 1953: restyled bumpers and overriders, full length chrome side strips, restyled bonnet motif, bonnet motif and chrome screen rubber inserts introduced on Consul, restyled interior trim including improved, colour-keyed rubber floorcovering on Consul, footrest alongside accelerator pedal, lower camber rear springs, flashing direction indicators in place of the semaphore type.

Convertible models now in production with prices of £808 for the Consul with manual hood, and £960 for the Zephyr Six on which a power operated hood was standard. No Zephyr Zodiac convertibles were being offered. Consul and Zephyr Six saloon prices unchanged at £666 and £754.

March 1954: Chrome plated top piston rings now fitted to Consul and Zephyr Six engines from numbers EOTA 129555 and EOTTA 80964. Narrow fan belts with appropriately modified dynamo and crankshaft pulleys introduced from numbers EOTA 130125 and EOTTA 81460.

June 1954: Original camber rear springs re-adopted from engine numbers EOTA 143842 and EOTTA 96111. Zodiac type rear spring insulators now fitted to Consul and Zephyr Six.

September 1954: Heavy duty rear shock absorbers on all models from engine numbers EOTA 154731 and EOTTA 105696. PVC headlining introduced on Zodiac, improved cloth headlining with a tighter weave now on Zephyr Six. Restyled rear lamps including reflectors on all models.

October 1954: Increase in range of rearward travel of front seat adjustment.

November 1954: Heater hose and temperature gauge take off points relocated forward on cylinder head. Cast aluminium flywheel cover plate replaced previous pressed-steel cover, involving changes to rear of cylinder block casting. New flywheel with dished front face,

and new longer clutch slave cylinder pushrod and retracting spring required due to thicker flywheel cover. Clutch pedal assist spring introduced on six-cylinder models only from engine number EOTTA 112432.

January 1955: New wheeltrim ring with flat cross-section introduced on Zodiac.

February 1955: Self-priming oil pump introduced from engine numbers EOTA 175035 and EOTTA 126427. Shroud type valve stem oil seals, in conjunction with shorter valve guides, replaced the valve stem oil seal rings from engine numbers EOTA 179775 and EOTTA 129225.

March 1955: Longer accelerator pedal pad on all models. PVC headlining introduced on Zephyr Six.

May 1955: Oil filled ignition coil on all models.

August 1955: Borg Warner overdrive available as optional extra on six-cylinder models only at £63.

October 1955: Separate amber flashing indicators at the rear in place of previous red indicators incorporated in rear lamp units. Front indicators remained white incorporated in front sidelamp unit.

November 1955: Purchase tax increase raised prices to £706, Consul (convertible £856), £799, Zephyr Six (convertible £1016), and £901 for the Zephyr Zodiac.

February 22nd 1956: Production ceased following the announcement of the Mk2 range the previous day.

Approximate mid-month engine numbers

Engine production was of course ahead of final vehicle assembly date, but as the chassis number corresponded to the engine fitted the following list is useful for identifying approximate car build date.

C O N S U L

1951	EOTA (4 cyl)	EOTTA (6 cyl)
January	0371	–
February	1410	008
March	3024	015
April	5411	048
May	7876	405
June	10025	1340
July	11950	3072
August	14190	4304
September	18138	4412
October	23100	--
November	28488	–
December	33297	4442

1952		
January	38641	4443
February	43838	4579
March	48076	5222
April	50772	6441
May	53134	8838
June	55715	11313
July	57540	12458
August	59053	13915
September	61169	16467
October	64266	19785
November	67513	23305
December	70613	26405

1953		
January	74089	29353
February	77864	32126
March	81951	35217
April	86321	38754
May	90876	41727
June	95281	46139
July	99819	50165
August	101884	53805
September	105213	57639
October	110376	62039
November	114961	66414
December	119128	70676

1954		
January	122677	74515
February	126636	78144
March	131305	82693
April	135687	87563
May	139872	92011
June	144314	96461
July	147990	100004
August	151203	102674
September	155050	105856
October	159647	109973
November	163714	114763
December	168370	119425

1955		
January	172864	124078
February	177390	128935
March	182017	134119
April	186658	138969
May	191149	143321
June	195946	148234
July	200607	152509
August	204303	156153
September	208899	160442
October	213788	164715
November	218876	168255
December	223834	171751

1956		
January	228797	173559
February	231905	175370

Car production ceased in February 1956. Engine production was greater than car total due to the need for occasional replacement engines for cars in service. in July 1953 both the four- and six-cylinder units were added to the Ford Exchange Engine Plan, in which the customer's original engine was taken in against a new or fully reconditioned engine at an exchange price of £31 for a Consul engine, and £42 for the six-cylinder units.

SPECIFICATION

Specification: Consul

Type	Ford Consul
Manufacturer's type designation	EOTA
Built	Dagenham, England. January 1951 – February 1956
Numbers made	231,481 (Includes convertibles and estate cars).
Engine:	
Cylinder block	Cast iron, deep-skirt extending below crankshaft centre line. Four cylinders in-line, water jacketing encircling each individual cylinder.
Cylinder head	Cast iron, with wedge-shaped combustion chambers and siamezed inlet ports. Separate valve guides.
Valve gear	Overhead, operated by pushrods and rockers from side-mounted camshaft.
Crankshaft	Cast alloy steel, counterbalanced and with main and big end journal overlap. Three main bearings.
Capacity	1508cc.
Bore & stroke	79.37mm x 76.2mm.
Compression ratio	6.8:1
Maximum power	47bhp at 4400rpm (nett).
Maximum torque	72lbs/ft at 2400rpm (nett).
Fuel system:	
Carburettor	Single Zenith downdraught incorporating an accelerator pump.
Fuel pump	AC mechanical, incorporating a vacuum pump for windscreen wiper operation.
Fuel tank capacity	9 gallons.
Transmission:	
Clutch	Hydraulic. Single dry plate, 8 inch diameter.
Gearbox	3-speed constant mesh. Synchromesh on second and top gears.
Rear axle	Hypoid, three-quarter floating. 4.625:1 ratio prior to February 1952. 4.556:1 ratio from February 1952 onwards.

Overall gear ratios:	4.625:1 axle	4.556:1 axle	
first	13.135	14.898*	12.939
second	7.598	7.704*	7.480
top	4.625	4.556	4.556
Road speed/1000rpm:			
first	5.24mph	4.67mph*	5.38mph
second	9.06	9.04*	9.3
top	14.9	15.3	15.3

(*Between November 1952 and April 1953 when lower indirect gearbox ratios were fitted).

Suspension:

Front — Independent by MacPherson struts incorporating hydraulic telescopic shock absorbers. Coil springs.

Rear — Non independent. Longitudinally mounted leaf springs of 7 leaves each. Lever arm hydraulic shock absorbers.

Steering — Worm and peg steering box mounted behind axle line. 13.6:1 ratio. 40ft 6in turning circle.

Brakes — Girling hydraulic. 9in diameter drums on all four wheels with two leading shoes in front drums, one leading shoe and one trailing in rear drums. 121sq.in total lining area.

Wheels and tyres — Pressed steel disc wheels, five stud fixing. Rim diameter 13in, rim width 4in. 5.90 x 13 tyres running at 28psi.

Electrical system — 12 volt positive earth, 45 ampere hour battery. Two brush generator, max output 228 watts, max charge rate 19 amps. Separate voltage control regulator.

Bodywork — 4-door saloon, all steel welded integrally constructed body/chassis unit, with bolt on wings and separate front panel. Built by Briggs Motor Bodies, Dagenham.
2-door convertible, built by Carbodies of Coventry on reinforced saloon floorpan.
Estate cars converted from ready-built saloons by E.D. Abbott, Farnham, Surrey.

Dimensions:

Overall length — 13ft 10in.
Overall width — 5ft 4in.
Height — 5ft 0.75in.
Wheelbase — 8ft 4in.
Track — 4ft 2in (front). 4ft 1in (rear).

Weight — 21.75cwt (saloon).

Performance (saloon):

Figures from *The Autocar* 22nd July 1955

Max speed: — 73mph(mean), 74mph(best).
2nd gear — 49mph.
1st gear — 29mph.
Acceleration:
0-60mph — 25.9 seconds
1/4 mile — 23.4 seconds (from standing start).
Top gear/2nd gear.
20-40mph — 12.1 sec./7.3 sec
30-50mph — 14.5sec./–
40-60mph — 17.8sec./–
Fuel consumption — 26 to 31mpg.

Specification: Zephyr Six & Zephyr Zodiac

Type — Ford Zephyr Six & Zephyr Zodiac.
Manufacturer's type designation — EOTTA.
Built — Dagenham, England. February 1951 – February 1956 (Zephyr Six), October 1953 – February 1956 (Zephyr Zodiac).
Numbers made — 152,677(Zephyr Six), 22,634(Zephyr Zodiac).

Engine:

Cylinder block	Cast iron, deep-skirt extending below crankshaft centre line. Six-cylinders in-line, water jacketing encircling each individual cylinder.
Cylinder head	Cast iron, with wedge shaped combustion chambers and siamezed inlet ports. Separate valve guides.
Valve gear	Overhead, operated by pushrods and rockers from side-mounted camshaft.
Crankshaft	Cast alloy steel, counterbalanced and with main and big end journal overlap. Four main bearings.
Capacity	2262cc.
Bore & stroke	79.37mm x 76.2mm.
Compression ratio	6.8:1(Zephyr Six), 7.5:1(Zephyr Zodiac).
Maximum power(nett)	68bhp at 4000rpm(Zephyr Six), 71bhp at 4200rpm(Zephyr Zodiac).
Maximum torque(nett)	108lbs/ft at 2000rpm(Zephyr Six), 112lbs/ft at 2000rpm(Zephyr Zodiac).

Fuel system:

Carburettor	Single Zenith downdraught incorporating an accelerator pump.
Fuel pump	AC mechanical, incorporating a vacuum pump for windscreen wiper operation.
Fuel tank capacity	9 gallons.

Transmission:

Clutch	Hydraulic, single dry plate, 8in diameter.
Gearbox	3-speed constant mesh, synchromesh on second and top gears.
Rear axle	Hypoid, three-quarter floating. 4.375:1 ratio prior to February 1952. 4.444:1 ratio from February 1952 onwards.

Overall gear ratios:	4.375:1 (to Feb 1952)	4.444:1 (from Feb 1952)	
first	12.425	14.531*	12.620
second	7.187	7.514*	7.297
top	4.375	4.444	4.444
Road speed/1000rpm:			
first	5.75mph	4.93mph*	5.68mph
second	9.95	9.55*	9.83(14.0)**
top	16.35	16.15	16.15(23.0)**

*Between November 1952 and April 1953 when lower indirect gearbox ratios were fitted. **Figures in brackets for Borg Warner overdrive.*

Suspension:

Front	Independent by MacPherson struts incorporating hydraulic telescopic shock absorbers. Coil springs.
Rear	Non-independent. Longitudinally mounted leaf springs of 7 leaves each. Lever arm hydraulic shock absorbers.

Steering

Worm and peg steering box mounted behind axle line. 13.6:1 ratio. 41ft 6in turning circle.

Brakes

Girling hydraulic. 9in diameter drums on all four wheels with two leading shoes in front drums, one leading shoe and one trailing in rear drums. 121sq. in total lining area.

Wheels and tyres

Pressed steel disc wheels, five stud fixing. Rim diameter 13in, rim width 4.5in. 6.40 x 13 tyres running at 24psi.

Electrical system

12 volt positive earth, 45 ampere hour battery (57 ampere hour on Zephyr Zodiac). Two brush generator, max output 228 watts, max charge rate 19 amps.
Separate voltage control regulator.

Bodywork	4-door saloon, all steel welded integrally constructed body/chassis unit, with bolt on wings and separate front panel. Built by Briggs Motor Bodies, Dagenham.
	2-door convertible (Zephyr Six only) built by Carbodies of Coventry on reinforced saloon floorpan.
	Estate cars converted from ready-built saloons by E.D. Abbott, Farnham, Surrey.

Dimensions:

Overall length	14ft 3³/₄in.
Overall width	5ft 4in.
Height	5ft 0³/₄in.
Wheelbase	8ft 8in.
Track	4ft 2in. front
	4ft 1in. rear
Weight (saloon)	23.25cwt (Zephyr Six), 23.75cwt (Zephyr Zodiac).

Performance (saloon):

	Figures from *The Motor* 3rd October 1951.
Max speed:	79.8mph (mean), 81.1mph (best).
2nd gear	50mph.
1st gear	29mph.
Acceleration:	
0-60mph	20.2 seconds.
S/S ¹/₄ mile	21.8 seconds.
	Top gear/2nd gear.
20-40mph	8.2 sec./5.7 sec.
30-50mph	9.4 sec./8.1 sec.
40-60mph	11.8 sec./–
50-70mph	16.0 sec./–
Fuel consumption	23.7mpg overall.

ROAD TESTS

The Motor 498 May 23, 1951.

The Motor Road Test No. 7/51

Make: Ford. **Type:** Consul Saloon.

Makers: The Ford Motor Co., Ltd., Dagenham, Essex.

Dimensions and Seating

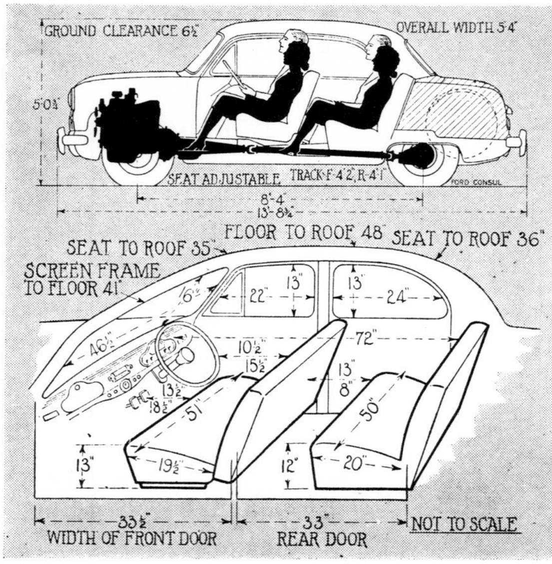
GROUND CLEARANCE 6½"
OVERALL WIDTH 5'4"
5'0¼"
SEAT ADJUSTABLE
TRACK F 4'2", R 4'1"
FORD CONSUL
8'-4"
13'-8¼"
SEAT TO ROOF 35"
FLOOR TO ROOF 48"
SEAT TO ROOF 36"
SCREEN FRAME TO FLOOR 41"
16½"
22"
13"
13"
24"
72"
46½"
10½"
15½"
13"
8"
13½"
18½"
51"
50"
13"
19½"
12"
20"
33½"
33"
WIDTH OF FRONT DOOR
REAR DOOR
NOT TO SCALE

Test Conditions

Warm, light wind; surface, dry tarmac; fuel, Pool petrol.

Test Data

ACCELERATION TIMES on Two Upper Ratios

	Top	2nd.
10–30 m.p.h.	11.9 secs.	6.8 secs.
20–40 m.p.h.	11.8 secs.	7.9 secs.
30–50 m.p.h.	14.0 secs.	—
40–60 m.p.h.	16.7 secs.	—
50–70 m.p.h.	24.4 secs.	—

ACCELERATION TIMES Through Gears

0–30 m.p.h	6.3 secs.
0–40 m.p.h.	10.7 secs.
0–50 m.p.h.	17.[illegible] secs.
0–60 m.p.h.	27.2 secs.
0–70 m.p.h.	41.8 secs.
Standing quarter mile	24.1 secs.

MAXIMUM SPEEDS

Flying Quarter Mile

Mean of four opposite runs	72.6 m.p.h.
Best time equals	74.4 m.p.h.

Speed in gears

Max. speed in 2nd gear	47 m.p.h.
Max. speed in 1st gear	29 m.p.h.

FUEL CONSUMPTION

36.5 m.p.g. at constant 30 m.p.h.
36.0 m.p.g. at constant 40 m.p.h.
30.5 m.p.g. at constant 50 m.p.h.
25.5 m.p.g. at constant 60 m.p.h.
Overall consumption (driven hard—see text) for 468 miles, 20 gallons=23.4 m.p.g.

INSTRUMENTS

Speedometer at 30 m.p.h.	4% fast
Speedometer at 60 m.p.h.	7% fast
Distance recorder	2% slow

WEIGHT

Unladen kerb weight	21¾ cwt.
Front/rear weight distribution	57/43
Weight laden as tested	25¼ cwt.

HILL CLIMBING (at steady speeds).

Max. top gear speed on 1 in 20	58 m.p.h.
Max. top gear speed on 1 in 15	52 m.p.h.
Max. gradient on top gear	1 in 12 (Tapley 185 lb./ton)
Max. gradient on 2nd gear	1 in 7.2 (Tapley 305 lb./ton)

BRAKES at 30 m.p.h.

0.90 g retardation (=33½ ft. stopping distance) with 130 lb. pedal pressure
0.85 g retardation (=35½ ft. stopping distance) with 100 lb. pedal pressure
0.70 g retardation (=43 ft. stopping distance) with 75 lb. pedal pressure
0.40 g retardation (=75 ft. stopping distance) with 50 lb. pedal pressure

In Brief

Price £425 plus purchase tax £237 12s. 4d. equals £662 12s. 4d.	
Capacity	1,508 c.c.
Unladen kerb weight	21¾ cwt.
Fuel consumption	23.4 m.p.g.
Maximum speed	72.6 m.p.h.
Maximum speed on 1 in 20 gradient	58 m.p.h.
Maximum top gear gradient	1 in 12
Acceleration	
10-30 m.p.h. in top	11.9 secs.
0-50 m.p.h. through gears	17.3 secs.

Gearing 14.5 m.p.h. in top at 1,000 r.p.m. 73 m.p.h. at 2,500 ft. per min. piston speed.

Specification

Engine	
Cylinders	4
Bore	79.37 mm.
Stroke	76.2 mm.
Cubic capacity	1,508 c.c.
Piston area	30.7 sq. in.
Valves	Push-rod o.h.v.
Compression ratio	6.8/1
Max. power	47 b.h.p.
at	4,400 r.p.m.
Piston speed at max. b.h.p.	2,200 ft. per min.
Carburetter	Downdraught
Ignition	12-volt coil
Sparking plugs	Champion NA8
Fuel pump	AC mechanical
Oil filter	AC full-flow
Transmission	
Clutch	8-in. s.d.p. with hydraulic control
Top gear (s/m)	4.625
2nd gear (s/m)	7.598
1st gear	13.145
Propeller shaft	Single open
Final drive	Hypoid bevel
Chassis	
Brakes	Girling hydraulic (2LS on front)
Brake drum diameter	9 ins.
Friction lining area	121 sq. in.
Suspension	
front	Coil-spring i.f.s.
rear	Semi-elliptic leaf
Shock absorbers	Armstrong hydraulic
Tyres	5.90×13
Steering	
Steering gear	Burman worm and peg
Turning circle	
right	41 feet
left	39½ feet
Turns of steering wheel, lock to lock	2¼
Performance factors (at laden weight as tested)	
Piston area, sq. in. per ton	24.3
Brake lining area, sq. in. per ton	96
Specific displacement, litres per ton-mile	2,460

Fully described in "The Motor," October 18, 1950.

Maintenance

Fuel tank: 9 gallons. **Sump:** 6½ pints (plus 1 pint for filter), S.A.E. 20 or 20W. **Gearbox:** 2 pints, S.A.E. 20 or 20W. **Rear axle:** 1⅞ pints, S.A.E. 90 hypoid. **Steering gear:** S.A.E. 90 E.P. **Radiator:** 16½ pints (2 drain taps). **Chassis lubrication:** By grease gun every 1,000 miles to 11 points, and every 5,000 miles to 2 points (universals). **Ignition timing:** 11° B.T.D.C. static. **Spark plug gap:** 0.032 in. **Contact breaker gap:** 0.012-0.014 in. **Valve timing:** I.O., 17° B.T.D.C.; I.C., 51° A.B.D.C.; E.O., 49° B.B.D.C.; E.C., 19° A.T.D.C. **Tappet clearances (cold):** Inlet and exhaust, 0.014 in. **Front wheel toe-in:** 1/16-1/8 in. **Camber angle:** 1 deg. 48 min. **Castor angle:** 0 deg. 30 min. **Tyre pressures:** Front 28 lb., rear 28 lb. **Brake (and clutch control) fluid:** Girling crimson. **Battery:** 12-volt., 45 amp./hr. **Lamp bulbs:** All 12-volt unless otherwise stated. Headlamps, 42/36 watt; side and rear number plate lamps, 6 watt; rear and stop lamps, 6/24 watt. Interior lamp and direction indicators (festoon), 6 watt. Instrument panel bulbs and warning lights for direction indicators, ignition, headlamp beam and oil pressure, all 16-18-volt, 3 watt.

Ref. B/16/51

B12

May 23, 1951. The Motor

—The FORD CONSUL

Latest Dagenham Product Reveals Remarkable Cornering Qualities, Good All-round Performance and Notable Ease of Control

SIMPLE STYLE—Carrying the minimum of ornamentation, the four-door, four-light body has a curved-glass rear window of notably generous area.

ADVANCED NEWCOMER—Tenacious road holding on corners is a striking characteristic of the Ford Consul to which the unusual I.F.S. layout doubtless contributes largely.

WHEN the Ford organization produces an entirely new model—as opposed to developing an existing basic type a stage further—one can expect to find evidence of original thinking. The very rarity of such an event is a guarantee that the designers have looked as far as possible into the foreseeable future, and planned accordingly. Technical originality is to be expected with, *ipso facto*, some flouting of convention.

The pair of Ford models (the 4-cylinder 1½-litre Consul and the 6-cylinder 2½-litre Zephyr) introduced at the Earls Court Motor Show last autumn, were entirely in keeping with what one expected in this direction. Now that an opportunity has been provided to test one of the Consul models over an extended mileage, it can be said without hesitation that the designers' ideas are entirely justified in practice.

New Standards

The Consul is a remarkable car and one which is not only likely to meet the motoring needs of a large section of the car-using public the world over, but, in some notable respects, is also likely to introduce the motoring man in the street to new standards of behaviour.

From the very moment of taking the wheel, one is conscious that the Consul is different. One sits, for example, farther from the facia board than is normal and surveys the road through a deep, curved screen placed farther forward in relation to the seat than is usual. The whole effect is one of spaciousness but there is also a suggestion of remoteness too. That, however, is belied by the good positioning of the controls which are neither cramped nor difficult to reach, whilst a further glance round shows that both wing con-

tours are visible; the all-round view to the sides and rear is also good—especially the latter, thanks to the large rear window. Through this, a well-placed tinted mirror provides a first-rate view.

To move off from rest is once again to experience that peculiar suggestion of remoteness, partly induced by the points already mentioned, but augmented by the very lightness and smoothness of the controls. As those who have studied the design will recall, both clutch and brake pedals are hung from the body side of the toe-board and take effect direct on master cylinders, from which the pedal movement is passed on by hydraulic means to the operating gear, thereby simplifying the layout and avoiding floor-board slots with the attendant difficulty of sealing them against noise, draughts and fumes. In the case of the clutch, this latest Girling arrangement also cuts out any need for complicated linkage designed to prevent movement of the flexibly mounted engine unit being transmitted to the pedal and produces unusually light and smooth engagement.

The same positive ease of movement attaches to the steering-column control for the 3-speed gearbox and the lever is conveniently placed to the left of the column near (but not too near) the pistol-grip handbrake. The steering, again, is notable for this same lightness of operation and the whole initial effect is to give the driver a peculiar sensation of remote control which he is not sure he is going to like.

In practice, a bare mile of driving serves to make up his mind for him. At the end of that distance, he not only feels entirely

at ease but realizes, if he has not experienced anything of the kind before, that the positive action of controls need not in any way be bound up with the effort required to operate them and that, for popular-priced cars at least, this Ford sets new standards in ease of control.

Outstanding Cornering

Having gained this confidence, a return of his original doubts may occur momentarily the first time his mounting confidence leads him into a corner rather faster than he intended. Then, for a brief second, the very lightness of the steering may produce a fleeting doubt as to whether the steering is really so good as he imagined, or whether the Consul is going to reveal itself as one of those cars (not uncommon in the thirties) in which light steering was achieved by a very undesirable degree of over-steer. His doubts will disappear in a further discovery—that the cornering characteristics of the Ford Consul are quite out of the ordinary.

Few cars, in fact, can rival the Consul in this most important respect. The steering, despite its lightness, is at all times positive and the car follows the course chosen with no noticeable over-steer or understeer tendencies; unless, moreover, one is pushing one's experiments to extreme limits, there is neither tyre howl nor roll. When the latter does

FULL-WIDTH LOCKER—An impression of the generous width of the luggage locker is given by the 2-gallon petrol can placed in the left-hand corner.

ANTI-DAZZLE—A rim around the simple instrument panel guards against reflections in the windscreen at night. The minor controls are conveniently grouped at the centre of the facia.

occur (on extreme provocation), it is strictly limited.

As readers will recall, the front suspension of the Consul is unique, the wheels being supported on vertical telescopic guides embodying both coil springs and shock absorbers : these guides are located at their upper ends in rubber-insulated conical roller bearings mounted in reinforced portions of the upper wing structures and, at their bases, by a combination of swinging arms and a special form of anti-roll bar. Despite its unconventionality, the system works with outstanding success in practice. If one can criticize the Consul on corners, in fact, it is the rear suspension, rather than the front which calls for comment, since some trace of rear-axle dither is occasionally noticeable when cornering very fast on bumpy roads; whilst the effect of this can definitely be felt, it produces no disconcerting results.

Besides providing outstanding cornering qualities, the suspension of the Consul also offers an extremely comfortable ride in which good bump absorption is coupled with an entire absence of pitch or float. One would, however, welcome a rather smaller turning circle for a car of this modest size.

Over 70 m.p.h. Maximum

With handling qualities of the order indicated, there is a strong temptation to drive the Ford Consul fast and, although this model is not intended in any way as a high-performance car (the larger-engined Zephyr being available for those who place the accent on performance), the Consul is, nevertheless, able to give a very good account of itself. With a maximum speed comfortably in excess of 70 m.p.h., it offers good all-round acceleration compared with the normal run of other machines in both its engine-size and its price classes.

The power unit is pleasantly flexible, is, in the main, very smooth and also conforms to a very acceptable standard of silence. On the debit side of the balance sheet is a noticeable vibration period on the over-run as the speed falls from about 27 m.p.h. to 22 m.p.h. and distinct evidence of body drumming which becomes noticeable, particularly in the rear seat, in the middle "sixties" but which largely disappears again as maximum speed is reached.

Accessibility for normal routine underbonnet maintenance is well planned,

especially in respect of the battery (which is placed alongside the engine) and, for the first time on this model, Ford owners have the advantage of overhead valves for easy maintenance.

In the matter of fuel consumption, the Consul, as the constant-speed figures given in the data panel indicate, is on a par with normal 1½-litre saloons and, in this connection, it must be stressed that the overall figure quoted included a high proportion of almost flat-out driving. At more restrained speeds, an appreciably higher figure than the 23.4 m.p.g. recorded could obviously be expected.

In accordance with usual Ford practice, the Consul has a 3-speed gearbox and there is no doubt that, for the average requirements of the average driver of this type of car, the ratios chosen are entirely adequate. Without wishing to introduce the age-old argument on the respective merits of three speeds or four, however, it would be idle to pretend that drivers used to 4-speed boxes do not miss having a third speed available for those occasions when it is desired to overtake other traffic after a serious check in cruising speed. As the 30-50 m.p.h. acceleration figure of 14 secs. indicates, the Consul is not in any way lacking in top-gear performance over this critical speed range but, equally obviously, it could do a great deal better with the aid of a ratio lower than the existing top but higher than second. The latter **gear** is good for a comfortable 35-40 m.p.h. and a rather overworked 47 m.p.h.

Another point on which one does not quite see eye to eye with the designers is in the omission, in a three-speed box, of synchromesh from bottom gear. Nowadays, drivers have become so accustomed to the assistance of this device that changing into a non-synchromesh gear on

the move (as one inevitably has to do in this case) calls for a mild degree of skill in double declutching which the present generation has either never learned, or largely forgotten. In other respects, the gearbox is above reproach with quiet gears and a baulking-ring synchromesh for top and second which gives foolproof as well as very rapid changes.

Of the general planning of the body, a certain amount has already been said. The interior has a plain simplicity which is not displeasing, with a painted facia board carrying a minimum of instruments (ammeter, fuel gauge and speedometer). Refinements such as arm rests are, understandably, omitted but, in the main, the seating is comfortable, although most drivers would welcome a more erect squab, whilst more headroom than the bare minimum provided in the rear would be an advantage. The rear seat itself is set unusually low in relation to the side windows and the front seat squab, with the result that child passengers find difficulty in seeing out, particularly forwards, unless they perch on the front of the seat.

Body Details

Finally, a few detail points: A novelty is the provision of a vacuum pump (incorporated in the base of the fuel pump) to operate the large-armed dual wipers, which thus continue to work irrespective of throttle opening and can be set to suit individual ideas on speed of operation . . the lights are of the latest (and now-familiar) Lucas double-dipping type . . . the luggage boot is roomy in spite of housing the spare wheel, but more accommodation for odds and ends within the car (there are no door pockets and only a small cubby locker) would be appreciated . . . the horn (if the example on the car tried is representative) is scarcely adequate for overtaking lorries . . . ventilation is well looked after by a combination of winding windows, hinged wide-opening panels on the front doors and a pair of controllable vents which distribute fresh air above the toe board . . . and both heater and radio can be obtained as extras.

In all, the Consul shows signs of eminently sensible detail planning which, in combination with its good all-round performance and quite exceptional handling qualities, make it that rare vehicle—an everyman's car that is basically good by any standard.

COMPACT—The short but wide compartment between the radiator bulkhead and the scuttle accommodates the 12-volt battery at one side of the engine, the optional interior heater at the other.

March 25, 1953.

The Motor Road Test No. 4/53

Make: Ford **Type:** Consul Saloon

Makers: Ford Motor Co., Ltd., Dagenham, Essex

Dimensions and Seating

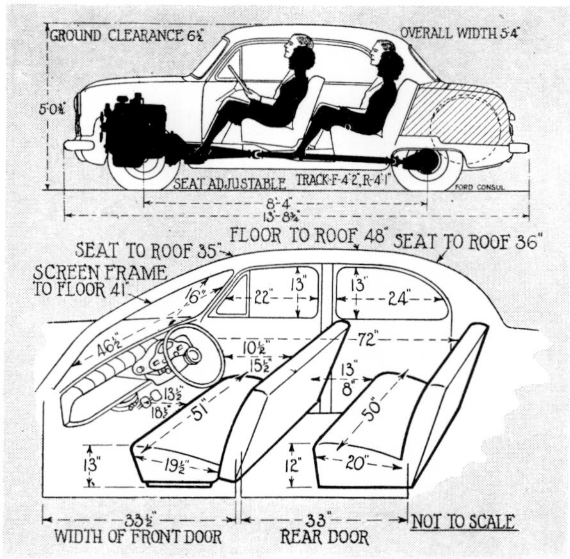
GROUND CLEARANCE 6¼"
OVERALL WIDTH 5'4"
5'0¼"
SEAT ADJUSTABLE
TRACK-F-4'2", R-4'1"
FORD CONSUL
8'-4"
13'-8¾"
SEAT TO ROOF 35"
FLOOR TO ROOF 48"
SEAT TO ROOF 36"
SCREEN FRAME TO FLOOR 41"
16"
22"
13"
13"
24"
46½"
10½"
15½"
72"
13"
8"
13½"
18½"
51"
50"
13"
19½"
12"
20"
33½"
WIDTH OF FRONT DOOR
33"
REAR DOOR
NOT TO SCALE

Test Conditions

Cold, light wind; surface, dry tarmac and concrete: Standard-grade fuel.

Test Data

ACCELERATION TIMES on Two Upper Ratios

	Top	2nd
10-30 m.p.h.	12.0 sec.	7.0 sec.
20-40 m.p.h.	12.0 sec.	7.4 sec.
30-50 m.p.h.	13.1 sec.	10.6 sec.
40-60 m.p.h.	18.6 sec.	—
50-70 m.p.h.	35.0 sec.	—

ACCELERATION TIMES Through Gears

0-30 m.p.h.	7.0 sec.
0-40 m.p.h.	11.8 sec.
0-50 m.p.h.	17.4 sec.
0-60 m.p.h.	28.0 sec.
0-70 m.p.h.	52.1 sec.
Standing Quarter Mile	23.8 sec.

FUEL CONSUMPTION

38.0 m.p.g. at constant 30 m.p.h.
36.0 m.p.g. at constant 40 m.p.h.
32.0 m.p.g. at constant 50 m.p.h.
26.0 m.p.g. at constant 60 m.p.h.
Overall consumption for 971 miles, 37.4 gallons = 26.0 m.p.g.

MAXIMUM SPEEDS
Flying Quarter Mile

Mean of four opposite runs	71.8 m.p.h.
Best time equals	75.0 m.p.h.

Speed in Gears

Max. speed in 2nd gear	56 m.p.h.
Max. speed in 1st gear	31 m.p.h.

WEIGHT

Unladen kerb weight	21¾ cwt.
Front/rear weight distribution	57/43
Weight laden as tested	25¼ cwt.

INSTRUMENTS

Speedometer at 30 m.p.h.	9% fast
Speedometer at 60 m.p.h.	11% fast
Distance recorder	4% fast

HILL CLIMBING (At steady speeds)

Max. top gear speed on 1 in 20	58 m.p.h.
Max. top gear speed on 1 in 15	53 m.p.h.
Max. gradient on top gear	1 in 11.1 (Tapley 200 lb./ton)
Max. gradient on 2nd gear	1 in 6.9 (Tapley 320 lb./ton)

BRAKES at 30 m.p.h.

0.93 g retardation (= 32½ ft. stopping distance) with 100 lb. pedal pressure
0.80 g retardation (= 37½ ft. stopping distance) with 75 lb. pedal pressure
0.53 g retardation (= 57 ft. stopping distance) with 50 lb. pedal pressure
0.23 g retardation (=131 ft. stopping distance) with 25 lb. pedal pressure

In Brief

Price £470 plus purchase tax £262 12s. 3d. equals £732 12s. 3d.

Capacity	1,508 c.c.
Unladen kerb weight	21¾ cwt.
Fuel consumption	26.0 m.p.g.
Maximum speed	71.8 m.p.h.
Maximum speed on 1 in 20 gradient	58 m.p.h.
Maximum top gear gradient	1 in 11.1.
Acceleration:	
10-30 m.p.h. in top	12.0 sec.
0-50 m.p.h. through gears	17.4 sec.

Gearing 15.1 m.p.h. in top at 1,000 r.p.m., 75.5 m.p.h. at 2,500 ft. per min. piston speed.

Specification

Engine

Cylinders	4
Bore	79.37 mm.
Stroke	76.2 mm.
Cubic Capacity	1,508 c.c.
Piston area	30.7 sq. in.
Valves	Pushrod o.h.v.
Compression ratio	6.8/1
Max. power	47 b.h.p.
at	4,400 r.p.m.
Piston speed at max. b.h.p.	2,200 ft. per min.
Carburetter	Downdraught
Ignition	12-v. coil
Sparking plugs	Champion N.8
Fuel Pump	AC mechanical
Oil filter	AC full-flow

Transmission

Clutch	8-in. s.d.p. with hydraulic control
Top gear (s/m)	4.556
2nd gear (s/m)	7.704
1st gear	14.898
Propeller shaft	Single open
Final drive	Hypoid bevel

Chassis

Brakes	Girling hydraulic (2LS on front)
Brake drum diameter	9 in.
Friction lining area	121 sq. in.
Suspension: Front	Independent, coil
Rear	Semi-elliptic leaf
Shock absorbers: Front	Armstrong hydraulic, direct acting
Rear	Double acting
Tyres	5.90-13

Steering

Steering gear	Burman worm and peg
Turning circle	40 feet
Turns of steering wheel, lock to lock	2½

Performance factors (at laden weight as tested)

Piston area, sq. in. per ton	24.3
Brake lining area, sq. in. per ton	96
Specific displacement, litres per ton mile	2,370

Fully described in "The Motor," October 18, 1950

Maintenance

Fuel tank: 9 gallons. **Sump:** 6½ pints (plus 1 pint for filter) S.A.E. 20 or 20W. **Gearbox:** 2¼ pints, S.A.E. 80 E.P. **Rear Axle:** 2½ pints S.A.E 90 hypoid. **Steering gear:** S.A.E. 90 E.P. **Radiator:** 16½ pints (2 drain taps). **Chassis lubrication:** By grease gun every 1,000 miles to 12 points. **Ignition timing:** 11° B.T.D.C. static. **Spark plug gap:** 0.032 in. **Contact breaker gap:** 0.012-0.014 in. **Valve timing:** I.O., 17° B.T.D.C.; I.C., 51° A.B.D.C.; E.O., 49° B.B.D.C.; E.C., 19° A.T.D.C. **Tappet clearances:** (Cold) Inlet 0.014 in., Exhaust 0.014 in. **Front wheel toe-in:** 1/16-1/8 in. **Camber Angle:** 1° 48 min. **Castor Angle:** 1° 30 min. **Tyre pressures:** Front 28 lb.; rear 28 lb. **Brake Fluid:** Girling crimson. **Battery:** 12-v. 45 a.h. **Lamp bulbs:** Headlamps, 42/36 w.; side and rear number plate lamps, 6 w.; rear and stop lamps, 6/24 w. Interior lamp and direction indicators (festoon), 6 w. Instrument panel bulbs and warning lights for direction indicators, ignition, headlamp beam and oil pressure, all 3 w.

Ref. B/16/53.

B12

March 25, 1953   THE MOTOR

—The Ford Consul

A Low-priced Family Car with Exceptionally Good Handling Qualities

THE 1½-litre Ford Consul was introduced at Earls Court in the autumn of 1950, and first road-tested by *The Motor* in the following May. Since then the manufacturers have followed the usual modern course in retaining the basic design over a number of years, making only such minor modifications as are found best to suit the average buyer. It is a tribute to the planners of the original Consul that visible modifications have been limited to a rearrangement of the facia, and that despite rising costs the Ford still falls in a price group well below that of most cars of similar size and performance.

Two years, however, not only bring many new prospective owners, but the interval is long enough for the car to be tested as a stranger and its merits weighed afresh. Incidentally on this occasion one of the testers had no previous experience of the car and the 1951 report was not referred to until a very considerable mileage had been covered and performance figures taken.

From a glance at the specification it would be fairly safe to assume that the owner of a Consul would be an everyday motorist requiring serviceability and generous passenger and luggage accommodation, ease of maintenance, and reasonable performance and economy, with less emphasis on the sports-car attributes of steering and roadholding. The four-cylinder, "over-square" engine develops 47 b.h.p. at 4,400 r.p.m., an adequate but not excessive power for a car capable of taking six passengers without too big a pinch.

It is only necessary to handle the car for a very short time to realize that it is in fact destined for two kinds of owner—the

family motorist and also the enthusiast with a limited depth of purse and a need for a really practical and reliable vehicle.

Exceptional Merits

From the driver's seat it is immediately apparent that the proportions are unlike those of most British cars. The windscreen is comparatively far forward, but this is soon taken for granted, and the large area swept by the wipers makes visibility in the rain better than in many cars of more orthodox dimensions. The steering wheel is also well away from the driver's chest, a position which allows very easy control without fatigue. The short bonnet is sensibly low and the raised wings are useful pointers for placing the car on the road or at the kerb.

In brief, any deviation from the normal so far as the external lines of the car are concerned is for the good, but inside things are not quite so happy. What the Americans call "lounge room," i.e. space from the pedals backwards to the leading edge of the rear seat, is somewhat less than normal so that some tall drivers might feel cramped on a long run even with the front seat pushed as far back as possible—a position which leaves only 8 inches of leg room for the rear seat passengers. A part of the problem is the encroachment of the

clutch housing into the body space which, in turn, gives the driver a limited choice of position for his left foot.

Both the enthusiast and the family man are quite at home within the first mile or two; almost as soon, in fact, as they have changed three gears and driven round a corner. The engine starts quickly with little use of the choke, although it was felt that first-time starting in any weather would depend on practice with any particular car. When warm the engine is very flexible for a four-cylinder of moderate size, and if one wishes to be lazy top gear can be engaged at an indicated ten or twelve miles per hour, although there is some pinking on the normal grade fuel for which the car supplied was stated to be tuned. Some vibration is noticeable on the overrun at speeds of about 45 m.p.h. and 30 m.p.h. in top gear, but the engine is otherwise silent almost to the limit of the speed range.

The gear-change is one of the best of the steering column type, the linkage being simplified by the use of only three forward gears. The short, stiff lever has a light and positive movement, and the syncromesh on the two upper ratios is so robust that it is virtually impossible to override, without any attempt to match the engine and transmission speeds. Clutch drag

COMPACT SEATING.— The front-seat view shows the comfortable angle of the steering wheel, wide parcels shelf and instruments shrouded to prevent reflection in the windscreen. Wide doors give easy access to the rear seats, in which passengers sit rather lower than is usual.

The Ford Consul · · · · · Contd.

DEEP VIEW. — The luggage locker is deep and roomy, and is illuminated by the twin rear number-plate lamps.

produces a slight "clonk" when bottom gear is engaged from standstill, but little practice is necessary to find this gear when the car is moving.

Apart from this feature the Girling hydraulically-operated clutch is excellent, with a light, smooth action completely insulated from engine vibration. No slip occurred even under the most arduous testing conditions.

In the course of a fortnight of English winter practically every kind of weather was encountered, and consequently every kind and condition of road surface, providing the best possible test of suspension. It will be recalled that the independent front suspension of the Consul is of unique design, with coil spring and shock absorber combined in one telescopic unit carrying the stub axle. Each unit is pivoted at its upper end in a rubber-insulated mounting inside the front wing (which is, of course, part of the integral body structure), and held at the bottom on a swinging arm and one end of the anti-roll bar. The uniqueness extends to performance as well as design, for in this instance the makers have not reached a compromise between soft springing to absorb road shocks and firm springing for stability on corners, but rather have combined the two.

Severe Tests

The suspension, including that at the rear by semi-elliptic leaf springs, is soft, and deals admirably with ordinary bad surfaces, of which the only indication is a certain degree of drumming through the body shell. Really severe conditions were also tried, over a couple of miles of unmade road in South Devon, involving continual ruts and pot-holes up to four inches deep with several stretches of deep mud. In contrast to the usual cautious approach with a non-independently sprung car, at a speed of perhaps 10 m.p.h., the Consul was driven straight down at 30 m.p.h. with no regard whatever for the hazards, which were felt only on the rare occasions when the springs reached the limit of their travel. It may be noted in passing that the muddy sections were taken downhill; the question of rear wheel adhesion will be mentioned later.

On more normal surfaces the Consul shows up in quite a different light, with the ability to take corners at speed in a manner formerly associated with much more expensive or less comfortable cars. The roll is small by modern standards, although passengers, if not the driver, may slide around somewhat on the bench-type

front seat, which, like the rest of the upholstery, is covered in P.V.C. and is not provided with a central armrest. This is perhaps a carping complaint if the Ford is considered as a family car, for the trouble is a direct result of its outstanding cornering powers. The steering is light and accurate, and there is no appreciable over- or under-steer. Again, the enthusiast might be critical of the feeling of "rubber joints" in the linkage, which does not lend itself to very quick movements of the wheel in emergency, but this is certainly no more accentuated than in the majority of current models, and in practice it is very easy to control incipient slides on a slippery surface.

The one serious criticism which must be made concerns this relative lack of adhesion of the back wheels. While of no account in dry weather or even on an ordinary wet road, the front-rear weight distribution of 57 : 43 does induce an uncomfortable degree of wheelspin when cornering or starting from rest on, for example, the wet wood-block surface often found in Central London.

The Girling hydraulic brakes are smooth and adequately powerful, fairly high pedal pressure being needed for a really quick stop. They show no tendency to fade under any but the most unusual provocation. The pistol-grip hand brake under the facia to the left of the steering column is strictly for parking only, and the angle could be improved by inclining it rather more to the left and downwards.

The restricted leg room which results from the inter-axle seating and a short wheelbase has already been mentioned. The seating position is otherwise good, and keeps the driver in a comfortable, upright position (with plenty of head room) which is not tiring on the longest journey. Visibility is excellent in all directions, aided

by a large rear window, but the driving mirror is unfortunately too small for the whole of this window to be seen without moving the head. An external mirror for fitting to the wing is obtainable as one of a number of standard accessories. A great improvement since the original Consul is the provision of a full-width parcels shelf on which the Ekco radio takes up very little room, while the instruments have been incorporated in a raised mounting over the steering column where they are seen with the minimum deflection of the eyes from the road. A fuel gauge and ammeter are provided, with a green warning light to indicate low oil pressure. It is disappointing to find a speedometer with a flatter of about 10% in place of the accurate instruments for which Ford products were once noted.

Details Analysed

The vacuum-operated windscreen wipers do not vary greatly in speed with the throttle opening, and the lights, controlled by a neat push-pull switch, are good enough for an indicated 60-65 m.p.h. on the open road.

Under-the-bonnet accessibility is all that is likely to be required by the average owner-driver who relies upon his service station for major repairs and maintenance. The battery is especially well placed for easy inspection and the dipstick can be reached without getting the hand and sleeve dirty or burnt, but the large heater unit and the coil tend rather to obscure the fuel pump. In view of the heavy air cleaner carried on top of the downdraught carburetter, this might well be strutted laterally against the vibration of the flexibly mounted engine.

The luggage locker is unusually roomy, and although the spare wheel is carried internally its small size makes removal a simple matter.

Comparison with the previous performance figures shows that the raised final drive ratio has brought a worthwhile improvement in fuel consumption, at the cost of a very slight drop in acceleration and maximum speed, hardly enough to worry even the keen driver, while the lower stressing of the engine and consequent reduction of both noise and wear will undoubtedly appeal to the man who motors because he has to. To either kind of owner the Consul represents quite remarkable value.

FORE AND AFT.—Functional simplicity is apparent in these two views of the Consul. There are useful wrap-around bumpers, but no unnecessary trimmings.

November 24, 1954

The Motor Road Test No. 31/54

Make: Ford   **Type:** Zephyr-Six Convertible

Makers: Ford Motor Co., Ltd., Dagenham, Essex

TRACK:— FRONT 4'- 2" REAR 4'- 1"
SEAT ADJUSTABLE
OVERALL WIDTH 5'- 4"
5'- 0¾"
GROUND CLEARANCE 6½" SCALE 1:50
8'- 8"
14'- 3¾"
FORD ZEPHYR SIX CONVERTIBLE

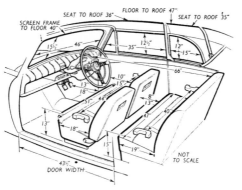

SEAT TO ROOF 36" FLOOR TO ROOF 47" SEAT TO ROOF 35"
SCREEN FRAME TO FLOOR 40"
46" 35" 12½" 12" 15"
15½"
13 18" 10"
51 44" 13" 8"
13" 40"
13" 18" 47"
15" 19"
66"
NOT TO SCALE
43½"
DOOR WIDTH

Test Data

CONDITIONS: Cool weather with strong diagonal wind. Smooth tarred road surface drying after rain. Standard grade pump fuel.

INSTRUMENTS

Speedometer at 30 m.p.h.	.. ..	3% fast
Speedometer at 60 m.p.h.	.. ..	5% fast
Distance recorder	.. ..	1% fast

MAXIMUM SPEEDS

Flying Quarter-mile

Mean of four opposite runs	..	79.8 m.p.h.
Best time equals	.. ..	81.1 m.p.h.

Speed in gears

Max. speed in 2nd gear	.. ..	50 m.p.h.
Max. speed in 1st gear	.. ..	30 m.p.h.

FUEL CONSUMPTION

31.5 m.p.g. at constant 30 m.p.h.
29.5 m.p.g. at constant 40 m.p.h.
26.0 m.p.g. at constant 50 m.p.h.
22.5 m.p.g. at constant 60 m.p.h.
18.5 m.p.g. at constant 70 m.p.h.
Overall consumption for 567 miles, 25.4 gallons, equals 22.3 m.p.g.
Fuel tank capacity 9 gallons.

ACCELERATION TIMES Through Gears

0-30 m.p.h.	.. .. ..	6.2 sec.
0-40 m.p.h.	.. .. ..	9.7 sec.
0-50 m.p.h.	.. .. ..	14.8 sec.
0-60 m.p.h.	.. .. ..	21.9 sec.
0-70 m.p.h.	.. .. ..	32.1 sec.
Standing Quarter Mile	..	22.3 sec.

ACCELERATION TIMES on Two Upper Ratios

		Top	2nd
10-30 m.p.h.	.. ..	9.1 sec.	5.8 sec.
20-40 m.p.h.	.. ..	9.5 sec.	6.6 sec.
30-50 m.p.h.	.. ..	10.1 sec.	9.4 sec.
40-60 m.p.h.	.. ..	12.4 sec.	—
50-70 m.p.h.	.. ..	18.7 sec.	—

HILL CLIMBING (At steady speeds)

Max. top gear speed on 1 in 20	..	69 m.p.h.
Max. top gear speed on 1 in 15	..	63 m.p.h.
Max. top gear speed on 1 in 10	..	52 m.p.h.
Max. gradient on top gear	..	1 in 7.8 (Tapley 285 lb./ton)
Max. gradient on 2nd gear	..	1 in 4.9 (Tapley 445 lb./ton)

BRAKES at 30 m.p.h.

0.85 g retardation .. (= 35½ ft. stopping distance) with 100 lb. pedal pressure
0.69 g retardation .. (= 43½ ft. stopping distance) with 75 lb. pedal pressure
0.39 g retardation .. (= 77 ft. stopping distance) with 50 lb. pedal pressure
0.18 g retardation .. (= 167 ft. stopping distance) with 25 lb. pedal pressure

WEIGHT

Unladen kerb weight	.. ..	23¾ cwt.
Front/rear weight distribution	..	59/41
Weight laden as tested	.. ..	27¼ cwt.

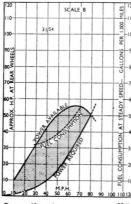

SCALE B
31/54
APPROX. H.P. AT REAR WHEELS
GALLONS PER 1,000 MILES
FUEL CONSUMPTION AT STEADY SPEED
POWER AVAILABLE
FUEL CONSUMPTION
POWER REQUIRED
M.P.H.

Drag at 10 m.p.h.	.. .. ..	38 lb.
Drag at 60 m.p.h.	.. .. ..	156 lb.

Specific Fuel Consumption when cruising at 80% of maximum speed (i.e. 63.8 m.p.h.) on level road, based on power delivered to rear wheels .. 0.83 pints/b.h.p./hr.

SCALE B
31/54
MAX. SPEED
M.P.H.
TOP GEAR
THROUGH GEARS
¼ MILE
TIME IN SECONDS

Maintenance

Sump: 8 pints, plus 1 pint in filter. S.A.E. 20. **Gearbox:** 2½ pints, S.A.E. 80 E.P. gear oil. **Rear Axle:** 2½ pints, S.A.E. 90 E.P. gear oil. **Steering gear:** E.P. gear oil. **Radiator:** 22 pints (2 drain taps). **Chassis lubrication:** By grease gun to 12 points and oil gun to 2 points every 1,000 miles. **Ignition timing:** Set according to mark on crankshaft nose 'pulley. **Spark plug gap:** 0.032 in. **Contact breaker gap:** 0.014-0.016 in. **Firing order:** 1-5-3-6-2-4. **Valve timing:** I.O., 17° B.T.D.C.; I.C., 51° A.B.D.C.; E.O., 49° B.B.D.C.; E.C., 19° A.T.D.C. **Tappet clearances:** (Hot) Inlet and Exhaust 0.014 in. **Carburetter settings:** Choke 27 mm., main jet 90, compensating jet 100. **Front wheel toe-in:** 0-⅛ in. **Camber angle:** + 0.5° to + 2°. **Castor angle:** + 0.5° to –0.5° **King pin inclination:** 2.75° to 4°. **Tyre pressures:** Front and rear, 24 lb. **Brake fluid:** EnFo. **Battery:** 12 volt, 45 amp. hr. **Lamp bulbs:** 12 volt: Headlamps 42/36 watt; Side/Direction indicators and tail/stop lamps 4/18 watt; rear direction indicators 18 watt; number plate lamps 5 watt.

Ref. B/23/54.

c16

—The Ford Zephyr-Six Convertible

An 80 m.p.h. Car Which is Both Tourer and Saloon

VERSATILITY is the most impressive characteristic of the Ford Zephyr-Six Convertible, which we have recently subjected to a formal Road Test in autumnal weather, but which we have also driven on other occasions during the spring and summer of 1954. This can be a roomy two-door saloon, seating four people in comfort, five or six people at a slight squeeze; in very quick time the front half of the roof can be folded to a "coupé de ville" position; merely pressing a switch lowers the roof the rest of the way, when the car becomes a fully open model with concealed hood, with four glass side windows which also disappear (complete with their frames) when the sun really shines. If the sun goes in, "coupé de ville" conditions can be restored without even stopping the car, and saloon snugness regained in very quick time.

Coachwork versatility such as this is an added attraction on a car which, as a saloon, has already earned a high reputation by providing versatility of performance which is outstanding in relation to a low purchase price. Any car bearing the name Ford is expected to be a thoroughly "sensible" vehicle and this model is no exception. Using low-grade fuel, with only slight pinking during acceleration from below 30 m.p.h., this is a smooth six-cylinder family car which will run very slowly or climb considerable hills in top gear. There are also, however, characteristics of performance and handling which have led many people to accept this model as a good substitute for a sports car—good acceleration and a maximum speed of virtually 80 m.p.h. should both be capable of some improvement with premium grade petrol.

Few Changes Needed

Inevitably, there has to be compromise over certain features of design, and on the Ford Zephyr-Six the transmission is the part of the car which is most clearly "touring" as distinct from "sports." This is a car which is intended to travel with the minimum number of gear changes per 1,000 miles, and so it has been given a relatively low top gear and a rather wide-ratio three-speed gearbox. Top gear can be used down to 10 m.p.h. when required and gives good acceleration away from this speed, but above 50 m.p.h. the engine begins to be audible and above 75 m.p.h. there is quite appreciable drumming.

For the average touring motorist the middle ratio of the gearbox will be noted as having clash-proof synchromesh to facilitate its engagement, as sufficing for any speed down almost to a standstill, and as being able to carry the car up a 1 in 5 gradient. The gears are reasonably quiet although not silent, and if needed with the car moving, the unsynchronized 1st gear is easy to engage. Those who buy this model on the basis of its high performance, however, will find that it is only up to 45 m.p.h., or a very little more, that 2nd gear provides faster acceleration than does top gear, and that especially from 1st to 2nd gear the powerful synchromesh mechanism discourages ultra-rapid changes of ratio.

First acquaintance with a new car often comes in a crowded garage or car park, and taking over a Zephyr-Six in these circumstances three things are immediately evident. Quite a high driving position gives a good forward view over a low bonnet which is flanked by prominent mudguards: the steering is reasonably light and quick even at low speeds: the turning circle is, however, substantially larger than is nowadays usual.

Away from confined quarters the limited steering lock ceases to be noticed, but a commanding driving position and easy steering remain as attractive features of the car. There is scarcely a trace of lost motion in the steering mechanism, so that the car can be placed accurately, although when overtaking other medium-speed traffic on cambered roads the Zephyr-Six does need driving rather consciously. Self-centring on corners, the steering is rather lacking in feel during straight-ahead driving, but an instant response to any need for sudden swerves inspires confidence.

Concentration of much weight on the front wheels means that, off the metalled road, the driving wheels will spin rather readily, and also that it is easier to skid the

In Brief

Price with leather upholstery: £687 plus purchase tax £287 7s. 6d. equals £974 7s. 6d.

Capacity	... ...	2,262 c.c.
Unladen kerb weight	...	23¾ cwt.
Fuel consumption	...	22.3 m.p.g.
Maximum speed	... ...	79.8 m.p.h.
Maximum speed on 1 in 20 gradient	... ...	69 m.p.h.
Maximum top gear gradient		1 in 7.8
Acceleration:		
10-30 m.p.h. in top	...	9.1 sec.
0-50 m.p.h. through gears		14.8 sec.

Gearing: 16.15 m.p.h. in top at 1,000 r.p.m.; 80.7 m.p.h. at 2,500 ft. per min. piston speed.

THE MOTOR

STOWAGE for the hood reduces the space available for luggage, but the boot remains a roomy and deep compartment from which the side-mounted spare wheel may be removed without disturbing luggage.

FULLY CLOSED, the convertible assumes the virtues of a weatherproof saloon, the large window areas avoiding the dark interior common to some drophead cars.

driving wheels by accelerating around a slippery corner than on other touring cars with less top-gear performance. This is, however, a car which naturally travels fast on winding roads as in addition to having rapid acceleration out of corners, it negotiates bends at quite high speeds without tyre squeal or appreciable roll: treated as a sports car, however, it does build up quite a large angle of roll and passengers on the bench-type seats become acutely conscious that they lack lateral support.

Avoiding the extremes of modern flexibility, the suspension gives good riding comfort over all kinds of surfaces, although at times slight shake suggests that the convertible body is a little less rigid than the all-steel saloon: actual rattles were almost entirely absent on the test model. Rear seat riding is very satisfactorily comfortable, although, as is usual, it is not so free from bumpiness as is the ride enjoyed by front seat travellers. Provision of a roof which folds completely out of sight involves narrowing of the rear seat and also some reduction of luggage space in the boot, but leaves the back seat comfortable for averagely tall men. Quarter windows provide lateral vision almost up to saloon standards, and the rear window is usefully

large, although unhappily it is rather below the level of the driving mirror.

Two large front-hinged doors are used, and the front seat backrest hinges forward in two halves to give access to the rear seat. Front seat access is easy and rear seat access not too awkward: the interior door handles are at the front of the doors, their inaccessibility from the back of the car being an advantage if children occupy the rear seats but a nuisance when adults are carried there.

As a closed car the Zephyr-Six convertible does not make it so easy to obtain ventilation without draughts as would the four-door saloon model: unfortunately the fresh-air heater delivers its heated air to the right-hand side of the car, warming the driver very much more than his passengers. Stage-by-stage opening of the body provides increasing amounts of fresh air and does not induce exaggerated amounts of back-draught such as can make some open cars very uncomfortable.

The Ford Zephyr-Six Convertible -   -

Extremely careful thought has obviously gone into most details of the convertible bodywork, as witness the neat folding of the plastic-covered top and the provision of double locks to secure each of the two heavy doors, although the window winders are rather indirect. To open the body to the "coupé de ville" position two knobs are unscrewed slightly, the centrally-hinged hood rails above the doors are folded and the roof "fabric" is rolled back and secured by two straps which have hitherto been held out of the way by two press-studs.

To lower or raise the roof after folding the front section it is merely necessary to press a switch down or up, when electro-hydraulic mechanism does the job neatly without it even being necessary to stop the car. Manual operation is possible should the powered system fail at any time. A hood cover is provided, but two surprising

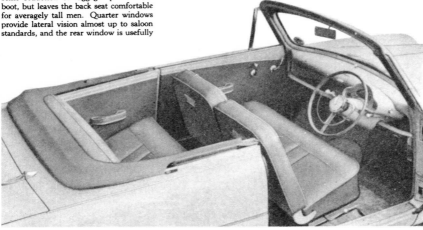

WIDE DOORS give access to the leather-upholstered interior of the test model (P.V.C. is available at reduced cost); the squab of the front bench seat is divided and hinged so that passengers have no difficulty in reaching the rear seat. Instruments are housed in a "binnacle" in front of the driver; a parcel shelf runs the width of the scuttle.

FULLY OPEN, the Zephyr-Six offers fresh-air-and-sun motoring, while winding side windows, swinging quarter-lights, and coupé de ville hood position are readily available to combat sudden weather changes.

------ Contd.

omissions are sun vizors and a car interior light—there is sufficient framing above the windscreen to allow both these items to be added as extras.

Our latest experience of this car allowed us to confirm that rain did not leak in anywhere, but was apt to be driven in through open windows. We also found that it started quite readily on frosty mornings although not warming up as quickly

SIX CYLINDERS and relatively low gearing make this car a flexible top-gear performer; features of the spacious under-bonnet compartment are a large air-cleaner, Zenith downdraught carburetter, side-mounted battery and a heater unit whose warmth is directed mainly towards the driver.

as do some other cars—premium-grade fuel speeded up this process. For a few minutes after a true cold start the gearchange was stiff to operate, thick gear oil being used in the gearbox, but this very soon became sufficiently warm to restore the usual light, smooth gear-lever movement.

Lights on this model are of the type usual in quantity-production British cars and gave quite good results. Vacuum-operated windscreen wipers, although far from quiet, proved well able to scrape drying mud off the curved glass; they slowed down when the engine was pulling hard, but a mechanical vacuum pump prevented them ever stopping completely. The optional heater already mentioned had useful power for British conditions, but the radio, although neatly planned and giving good tone, did not prove powerful enough to combat rather considerable wind noise at the high speeds which many

Zephyr owners use. Rather small in size, the brakes were smooth and progressive in touring usage, and were fully equal to an emergency stop from high speed, but repeated hard usage could heat them up quite quickly.

Emphasis has up to now been laid upon the performance of the Ford Zephyr-Six, a point to note being that the four-door saloon is rather lighter than the convertible model. Economy of operation depends very much upon driving methods, and our overall figure of 22.3 m.p.g.

includes, as usual, long distances of quite hard driving. Not dawdling by any means, running up to 60 m.p.h. at times, but refraining from using the gearbox unnecessarily, we covered 150 brisk miles on almost exactly six gallons of petrol to give an average of 25 m.p.g. Backed by the well-known Ford service organization, this should not be a very expensive car to run.

For a keen motorist, it is always difficult to reconcile conflicting wishes and needs to find one car which will suit all moods. The Ford Zephyr-Six convertible is an extremely attractive all-purpose model which is virtually without any direct rival in its field: a flexible and reasonably quiet saloon, a fast business car, an open tourer in which a whole family can enjoy healthy fresh air, and something akin to a sports car as well, it is a jack-of-all-trades with much to commend it.

Mechanical Specification

Engine

Cylinders	... ...	6
Bore	... ...	79.37 mm.
Stroke	... ...	76.2 mm.
Cubic capacity	... ...	2,262 c.c.
Piston area	... ...	46.0 sq. in.
Valves	... ...	Pushrod o.h.v.
Compression ratio	... ...	6.8/1
Max. power	... ...	68 b.h.p.
at	... ...	4,200 r.p.m.
Piston speed at max b.h.p.		2,100 ft. per min.
Carburetter	...	Zenith downdraught
Ignition	... ...	12-volt coil
Sparking plugs		Champion N8B, 14 mm.
Fuel pump	... ...	AC mechanical
Oil filter	... ...	AC full-flow

Transmission

Clutch	Single dry plate (hydraulic control)	
Top gear (s/m)	... ...	4.444
2nd gear (s/m)	... ...	7.297
1st gear	... ...	12.62
Propeller shaft	...	Open
Final drive	...	Hypoid bevel
Top gear m.p.h. at 1,000 r.p.m.		16.15
Top gear m.p.h. at 1,000 ft./min. piston speed		32.3

Chassis

Brakes	Girling hydraulic, 2 l.s. front	
Brake drum diameter	...	9 in.
Friction lining area	...	121 sq. in.
Suspension:		
Front	Coil spring I.F.S., with anti-roll torsion bar	
Rear	... ...	Semi-elliptic
Shock absorbers:		
Front	... Telescopic, incorporated in i.f.s.	
Rear	...	Piston type hydraulic
Tyres	... ...	6.40 - 13

Steering

Steering gear	...	Burman worm and peg
Turning circle	Left 42 feet.	Right 42 feet
Turns of steering wheel, lock to lock		2¼

Performance factors (at laden weight as tested):

Piston area, sq. in. per ton	...	33.8
Brake lining area, sq. in. per ton		89
Specific displacement, litres per ton mile	... ...	3,080

Fully described (saloon model) in *The Motor*, October 18, 1950.

Coachwork and Equipment

Bumper height with car unladen:
Front (max.) 23½ in., (min.) 14 in.
Rear (max.) 24 in., (min.) 14½ in.

Starting handle	No
Battery mounting ...	On left of engine
Jack	Ratchet handle screw jack
Jacking points ...	2 external sockets on each side of body

Standard tool kit: Tool bag, 2 double-ended spanners, spark plug spanner, cylinder head nut spanner, brake adjusting spanner, box spanner, adjustable spanner, screwdriver, pliers, grease gun, jack, wheel brace, tyre levers.

Exterior lights: 2 headlamps, 2 sidelamps/direction indicators, 2 stop/tail/direction indicator lamps.

Direction indicators: Flashing type, self cancelling.

Windscreen wipers: Twin blade, self parking, vacuum operated, with engine-driven vacuum booster pump.

Sun vizors	Nil

Instruments: Speedometer with non-trip decimal distance recorder, fuel contents gauge, ammeter.

Warning lights: Dynamo charge, oil pressure, headlamp main beam, direction indicators.

Locks:	
With ignition key ...	Ignition, both doors, luggage locker
With other keys	Nil
Glove lockers	Nil
Map pockets	Nil
Parcel shelf	Beneath facia panel
Ashtrays	1 front, 2 rear
Cigar lighters	Nil
Interior lights	Nil
Interior heater ...	Optional extra, fresh air type with windscreen de-misters
Car radio ...	Optional extra (Ekco)

Extras available: Heater, radio; also full range of "EnFo" extras available from Ford agents.

Upholstery material	Leather (P.V.C. plastic at £10 less basic price)
Floor covering	Carpet

Exterior colours standardized: Winchester blue, Westminster blue, Canterbury green, Dorchester grey, Ivory, Black. (For export only, Mandarin red also available).

Alternative body styles: 4-door saloon, 4-door "Zodiac" de luxe saloon.

Available in several different colour combinations, the dual scheme that is a feature of the Zephyr Zodiac has the effect of making it look smaller than in fact it is. In this instance the white wall tyres add a finishing touch. This particular car was in cream and blue. The name motifs at front, side and rear of the Zodiac are in 9-carat gold-plated zinc alloy.

The Autocar
ROAD TESTS

No. 1537:

FORD ZEPHYR ZODIAC SALOON

WHEN first introduced in the last half of 1950, the Ford Zephyr, with its six-cylinder pushrod overhead valve engine and coil spring independent front suspension, proved at once to be a winner. A lively performance and good roadholding always provide a popular combination and the Zephyr offered these qualities from the start, backed by the well-known world-wide Ford service organization. The Zephyr saloon in its standard form is supplied fitted with the normal equipment required by law in Great Britain and the customer has a very reasonable choice of body colour. He is able, as any car

owner is, to equip his Zephyr with numerous accessories to increase the comfort and help towards more pleasant motoring.

As the war years and their effects recede into the background, the material situation becomes easier for the car manufacturer and customers begin to demand more accessories and a greater choice of colour schemes. Some are prepared, and prefer, to add equipment to their cars gradually—for instance, when it is found that a new type of fog lamp has been introduced or a screen washer is required. There is the other type of owner who prefers to purchase his car already equipped with those extras which go a long way towards making motoring a little easier or more pleasant.

So the Zephyr Zodiac was introduced at the 1953 Earls Court Show and it is interesting to reflect that it is produced by the firm whose founder is credited with saying that the customer could have his car any colour he liked so long as it was black! In mechanical and structural specification the Zodiac is similar to the standard Zephyr, the notable difference being the compression ratio, which is 7.5 on the Zodiac as against 6.8 to 1 on the standard engine. The high-compression head and its valve cover are painted red for identification purposes. Apart from this the design is not

The twin exterior mirrors, and fog and long range driving lamps, are extremely useful standard fittings on the Zodiac. Flashing turn indicators are incorporated in the side and rear lamps.

82

ROAD TEST continued

Instruments and switches are placed at various points on the "control tower" round the steering column. The T-spoked steering wheel allows a clear view of the speedometer. Lighting switches and starter button are on the right-hand side and there is a small cubby hole below the right-hand corner of the facia, as well as a large one to the left.

altered, the unit body-frame being used with the clever coil spring independent front suspension having the dampers inside the springs; normal half-elliptic springs are used at the rear. Since the last Road Test by *The Autocar* of a Ford Zephyr the axle ratio has been raised slightly to 4.44 to 1. Previous overall ratios were 4.375, 7.187 and 12.434 to 1, so the use of a higher compression ratio, giving a b.h.p. of 71 at 4,200 r.p.m., compared with 68 at 4,000 for the earlier and also present standard Zephyrs, gives the Zodiac better acceleration all through the range and a slightly higher maximum speed. Also, since the last test occurred, higher octane rated fuels have been introduced, of which the engine designer has taken advantage.

The engine is extremely flexible and pulls strongly from below 12 m.p.h. in top gear up to its very creditable maximum without the slightest sign of roughness or vibration. When required, the majority of main road hills can be stormed in a very heartening fashion, while if the car is baulked on a gradient the use of second gear in the three-speed box enables it to overtake other vehicles in a fast and safe manner. Most satisfyingly, the engine responds immediately to quick throttle openings and if maximum power is used when accelerating on wet roads the comparatively small diameter wheels will spin. In spite of care during the take off, in an endeavour to obtain the best possible figures, wheelspin was noticeable during the standing start acceleration tests, and this on a dry

Ease of entry to both seats is a good feature of this British Ford. Check straps hold the doors in the open position. Arm rests form door pulls and the locks have an external push button action. A jacking socket is provided close to each wheel.

concrete surface. In addition to the excellent acceleration characteristics of the Zodiac, which are such a valuable feature of a car in these days of road congestion, it will cruise without effort at a genuine 70 m.p.h. when carrying three large passengers and a full complement of luggage.

Throughout the speed range there is no unpleasing mechanical noise or power roar from the engine, and, according to the way in which it is driven, it can be very economical for its size. Full and constant use of the performance will play ducks and drakes with fuel economy, but on one occasion during the test a consumption figure approaching 30 m.p.g. was achieved. Two factors contributed to this: the car was driven at speeds not exceeding 40 m.p.h. and the tyre pressures had been increased from the recommended figure of 24 to 32lb per sq in to lessen tyre squeal when cornering.

Most gradients, except those liable to be met off the beaten track, can be taken in second gear and the owner is reassured by the knowledge that there can indeed be few hills that the Zodiac would not clear in this useful intermediate gear. On all occasions during the test the engine responded immediately to the starter and very little use of the choke was required after a night in the open, with the radiator facing an east wind.

Good Gear Change

With the very useful top gear performance that is available, no great advantage is gained in normal circumstances by changing to second gear, except, for instance, when maximum acceleration is required for overtaking purposes. When it is necessary to change gear, the short, stiff, steering column mounted lever makes the operation a pleasure. There is no lost motion in the gear change mechanism and the synchromesh on second and top is good; very quick changes can be made in both directions without beating the synchromesh. The single-plate clutch has hydraulic operation and the take up is smooth, but the pedal movement required more effort than is usual in these days.

As the engine performance of cars tends to increase, so the designer has to ensure that the suspension will be firm enough to prevent the car rolling when driven at high speeds, and soft enough to absorb all shocks if the vehicle is taken along unmade roads such as occur overseas or in exceptional circumstances in Great Britain. The products of the Ford Motor Company have always had a reputation for being able to go anywhere, and, with the latest Ford design of independent front suspension, the Zephyr Zodiac gives the driver and passengers an excellent ride in all circumstances. It handles well on all surfaces and when deliberately provoked on a wet road the tail end showed no tendency to break away. The ride in the back seat is very good and it is quite possible for two people to fall asleep in the rear compartment when the car is cruising at quite high speeds.

The steering is positive and light and the car will follow

the line that is chosen without upsetting the driver's calculations. A very slight amount of understeer gives confidence and the car feels as safe on wet main roads at speed as it does on winding, badly surfaced by-roads. Tyre squeal was noticeable when cornering at even moderate speeds on some surfaces and experimenting with tyre pressures did not eliminate this.

The driving position promoted by the wide bench type seat is helped greatly by the extremely good vision the driver has. The whole of the top line of the left-hand front wing can be seen and the car can be driven through narrow gaps with safety and confidence—confidence that is gained almost at once by a driver strange to the car. The driving position is somewhat upright and does not compare favourably in comfort with that provided by the rear seat on a long journey. The thin-rimmed steering wheel is nicely placed and it is possible to operate the gear lever and the half-horn ring without removing the left hand completely from the wheel. The taller driver will find that the adjustment for the front seat is limited; the adjusting lever can be easily reached from the seat. The three pedals are of the pendant type and with right-hand drive there is ample room for the left foot away from the clutch pedal. Both foot and hand brakes are well up to their work. The brakes showed no signs of fade or inequality after the severe brake testing procedure and were well able to cope with any situation on the road. The pull-and-push hand brake lever, situated to the left of the steering column, can be reached by a tall driver without stretching forward when the seat is right back and the brake will hold the fully laden car on a severe gradient.

To a public accustomed to single-colour bodywork and whose taste in most things is almost world renowned for being conservative, the bright but not overpowering colour

FORD ZEPHYR ZODIAC SALOON

WHEELBASE	8' 8'
FRONT TRACK	4' 2'
REAR TRACK	4' 1'
OVERALL LENGTH	14' ·3·8'
OVERALL WIDTH	5' 3·9'
OVERALL HEIGHT	5' 0·75'

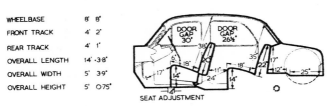

SEAT ADJUSTMENT

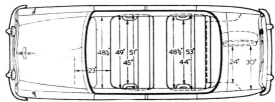

Measurements in these ½in to 1ft scale body diagrams are taken with the driving seat in central position of fore and aft adjustment and with the seat cushions uncompressed.

PERFORMANCE

ACCELERATION: from constant speeds. Speed Range, Gear Ratios and Time in sec.

M.P.H.	4.44 to 1	7.29 to 1	12.62 to 1
10—30 ..	7.9	5.1	4.5
20—40 ..	8.5	5.6	—
30—50 ..	9.6	7.9	—
40—60 ..	11.8	—	—
50—70 ..	15.3	—	—

From rest through gears to:

M.P.H.	sec.
30	5.4
50	13.5
60	20.4
70	29.7

Standing quarter mile, 21.5 sec.

SPEEDS ON GEARS:

Gear		M.H.P. (normal and max.)	K.P.H. (normal and max.)
Top ..	(mean)	80.2	129.1
	(best)	84	135.2
2nd ..	..	42—57	68—92
1st ..	..	22—31	35—50

TRACTIVE RESISTANCE: 30 lb per ton at 10 M.P.H.

TRACTIVE EFFORT:

	Pull (lb per ton)	Equivalent Gradient
Top	235	1 in 9.5
Second..	373	1 in 5.9

BRAKES:

Efficiency	Pedal Pressure (lb)
88 per cent	100
73 per cent	75
53 per cent	50

FUEL CONSUMPTION:
23.7 m.p.g. overall for 309 miles (11.9 litres per 100 km).
Approximate normal range 21-28 m.p.g. (13.5-10.1 litres per 100 km).
Fuel, first grade.

WEATHER: Dry, light breeze.
Air temperature 64.8 deg F.
Acceleration figures are the means of several runs in opposite directions.
Tractive effort and resistance obtained by Tapley meter.
Model described in *The Autocar* of October 23, 1953.

SPEEDOMETER CORRECTION: M.P.H.

Car speedometer:	10	20	30	40	50	60	70	80	90
True speed:	9.5	18.5	28	37	47	57	66	75.5	84

DATA

PRICE (basic), with saloon body, £600. British purchase tax, £251 2s 6d. Total (in Great Britain), £851 2s 6d. Extras: Radio, £47 17s 1d.

ENGINE: Capacity: 2,262 c.c. (138 cu in). Number of cylinders: 6. Bore and stroke: 79.37 × 76.2 mm (3.125 × 3.00 in). Valve gear: Overhead; pushrods and rockers. Compression ratio: 7.5 to 1. B.H.P.: 71 at 4,200 r.p.m. (B.H.P. per ton laden 51.9). Torque: 112 lb ft at 2,000 r.p.m. M.P.H. per 1,000 r.p.m. on top gear, 16.15.

WEIGHT (with 5 gals fuel): 23¾ cwt (2,660 lb). Weight distribution (per cent): F, 58; R, 42. Laden as tested: 27¼ cwt (3,060 lb). Lb per c.c. (laden): 1.3.

BRAKES: Type: F, Two-leading shoe; R, Leading and trailing. Method of operation: F, Hydraulic; R, Hydraulic. Drum dimensions: F, 9in diameter; 1.75in wide. R, 9in. diameter; 1.75in wide. Lining area: F, 60.5 sq in. R, 60.5 sq in (88 sq in per ton laden).

TYRES: 6.40—13in. Pressures (lb per sq in): F, 24; R, 24 (normal).

TANK CAPACITY: 9 Imperial gallons. Oil sump, 8 pints. Cooling system, 23¼ pints.

TURNING CIRCLE: 41ft 6in (L and R). Steering wheel turns (lock to lock): 2¼.

DIMENSIONS: Wheelbase: 8ft 8in. Track: F, 4ft 2in; R, 4ft 1in. Length (overall): 14ft 3.8in. Height: 5ft 0.75in. Width: 5ft 3.9in. Ground clearance: 7.1in. Frontal area: 20 sq ft (approximately).

ELECTRICAL SYSTEM: 12-volt; 57 ampère-hour battery. Head lights: Double dip; 42-36 watt bulbs.

SUSPENSION: Front, Independent; direct operation coil springs. Rear, Half-elliptic leaf springs. Anti-roll bar embodied in front suspension.

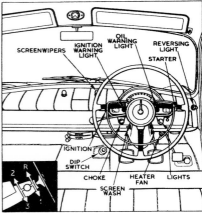

84   THE AUTOCAR, 16 JULY 1954

ROAD TEST . . . . continued

schemes available on the Zephyr Zodiac have brought new life to the roads of Britain and other countries. The equipment which is standard is well placed and not overdone. A long-range lamp and a pass or fog light supplement the head lamps, which themselves could be more powerful for fast night driving.

Two external wing mirrors give the driver a full view along both sides of the car and are cleverly spring loaded on their mountings, so that if accidentally knocked against they will spring back into position without having to be reset. In addition a large interior mirror gives a good rearward view through the back window. The well-placed and good-sized electric clock above the centre of the windscreen is lit at night, and the reversing lamp, controlled by a self-illuminating switch as required by law, the windscreen washer and a cigarette lighter are all items which are extremely useful in the appropriate circumstances. The white wall tyres, although they may not be everybody's choice, blend well with the paintwork and have the capacity of teaching some drivers not to be "kerb scrapers." Chromium plated wheel rims are also supplied as standard.

Light Interior

The interior finish of the bodywork balances the exterior and the occupants have an impression of a well-lighted, spacious compartment. The seats are covered with dual-tone hide and give ample support. Opening quarter lights are provided in the leading edges of the front windows and each door has an arm rest-cum-door pull. The arm rest on the driving side door is awkwardly placed for some drivers and tends to restrict arm movement. The facia is well laid out with a deep parcel shelf running from the left side to the steering column housing and a smaller compartment on the right. There are no pockets in the doors.

The instruments, consisting of the semicircular speedometer dial, fuel contents gauge and either temperature gauge or ammeter, are easily read from the driving seat and sufficiently well lit at night. At first sight the control switches may seem to have been thrown at the column housing and fixed in the positions they hit, but after a while the driver realizes the advantages of the irregular positioning of the controls over the more usual in-line all-alike method. Instead of a straight row of round knobs which have to be fumbled at in the dark, the control switches of the Zephyr Zodiac have been placed well apart, and after short acquaintance with the car the driver is able to place his hand on the required control immediately instead of wondering whether he is going to pull out the fog lamp switch instead of the windscreen wiper control which he may require at that moment.

In addition to a large ashtray in the centre of the facia, there is a smaller one in the back of the front seat and two adjustable sun vizors are placed above the windscreen, that on the passenger's side having a vanity mirror in the back. The fresh air heating and demisting unit is placed alongside the engine with the controls below the centre of the parcels shelf. Two vents above the facia direct hot or cold air on to the windscreen and the air pressure is supplemented by a fan controlled by a switch to the right of the steering column housing.

There are not likely to be complaints here about lack of space, though the locker is of somewhat irregular shape. A small tool compartment with a lid is provided between the spare wheel and the wing. Red reflectors are incorporated in the rear lamps, and a locking petrol filler cap is a standard fitting.

Additional air for the interior is controlled by a knob on the extreme left of the parcels shelf.

A radio can be supplied as an extra and when this is fitted the Zodiac owner can be satisfied that his car is as fully equipped as is really necessary. The control unit on the car tested fitted neatly below the centre of the facia, with one speaker unit in the left-hand corner of the shelf and a supplementary speaker with separate volume control sunk in the useful wide shelf behind the back seat. The extending aerial is placed in the rear edge of the right-hand front wing and can be extended without the driver having to leave the car.

Luggage Space

Below the bonnet the six-cylinder engine fits snugly amongst its auxiliaries and full marks must be given for the accessibility of the oil filler and the oil level dipstick. The dual Windtone horns, which have a powerful note, are fixed to the underside of the bonnet, which is held in the open position by a single strut. There is space for a large amount of luggage in the rear locker, which also houses the spare wheel in an upright position. The nine-gallon petrol tank is placed below the floor of the locker; the filler orifice, with its acute bend, will not take full flow from the average garage pump. A tool locker is provided for the small tools, but there is no fixed location for the jack and wheel brace, and no starting handle is provided. The simple two-legged jack with its ratchet handle works well and raises the car sufficiently for the wheels to clear the wing valances. There are 12 lubrication points which require attention every 1,000 miles.

Customary reaction to the Zodiac is that of admiration, and the owner who likes to have a car that is distinctive, as well as lively in performance, can consider the price difference between the standard Zephyr Six and the Zephyr Zodiac to be well worth while.

Battery, brake and clutch operation fluid reservoir, engine oil filler and radiator filler cap are all extremely easy to reach. The water container for the windscreen washer is placed against the bulkhead, behind the battery, while the fresh air and heater unit is concentrated on the opposite side of the compartment.

The arrangement of carburettors and inlet and exhaust manifolds is efficient and neat. There are two exhaust manifolds, each serving three cylinders and having its own down pipe.

FASTEST ZEPHYR YET?

SIX PORT ALLOY HEAD IS BASIS OF NEW RAYMOND MAYS CONVERSION

FOR some time Raymond Mays and Partners, Ltd., of Bourne, Lincolnshire, have been offering a Ford Zephyr conversion in which three carburettors were used. Now they have introduced a new conversion based on a two-carburettor, six-port alloy cylinder head made by the Rubery Owen organization. The results are such as to make a Zephyr converted in this way a very potent car indeed. At a compression ratio of 8.2 to 1 the converted engine gives over 100 b.h.p. compared with the 68 of the standard model.

The six inlet ports are fed by two S.U. carburettors, and the exhaust is collected from the six exhaust ports by two cast iron manifolds, to each of which is attached a down pipe. Two types of silencers, both made by Burgess, are available. Both have two inlets for the down pipes, but one has a single outlet and the other two. The latter, which was fitted to the car which *The Autocar* has tested, is distinctly noisy, the general sound effect being that associated with powerful sports cars. The other is very much quieter, and in a brief run in a car so equipped it was noted that the sound level was little higher than that of the standard car. The quieter system has not yet been bench tested, but it is not expected to detract much from the performance of the converted car.

The car tested was fitted with the Laycock-de Normanville overdrive, which provided, in effect, five gears instead of the usual three. But as this equipment is **not** part of the Mays' engine conversion it was not used in obtaining the performance data shown on this page. Apart from the overdrive, the performance is truly impressive; for example, 70 m.p.h. can be reached from a standstill in 18.3sec, compared with 32.1sec for the standard Zephyr. In top gear the time taken to reach 60 m.p.h. from 40 m.p.h. is 7.4 instead of 11.9sec. Also, 80 m.p.h. can be reached from rest in 23.7sec—yet this speed

Speeds through the gears m.p.h.	Standard Zephyr	Zephyr Zodiac	Mays Conversion
0—30	5.5	5.4	4.0
0—50	14.1	13.5	9.4
0—60	21.1	20.4	13.2
0—70	32.1	29.7	18.3
0—80	—	—	23.7
Top gear m.p.h.			
20—40	9.2	8.5	7.2
40—60	11.9	11.8	7.4
Standing ¼-mile	—	21.5	18.9

The figures for the standard Zephyr and Zodiac are extracted from *The Autocar* Road Tests.

is virtually the maximum of the standard and Zodiac models.

The highest speed achieved during the test was 95 m.p.h. (with the use of the overdrive). At this speed the car was still accelerating, if only slightly, and it is very likely that it could top 100 m.p.h. in favourable conditions. The Mays company rightly avoids over-emphasizing top speed, relegating its usefulness to boasting to one's friends! For it must be realized that the brakes, transmission, and so on, of the Zephyr were not designed for three-figure speeds. The attraction of the conversion lies in the vastly improved power

where it is most useful—in the 30 to 80 m.p.h. range.

The overdrive is very enjoyable in conjunction with the cylinder head conversion, although the two modifications are not linked. The five gears, coupled with the extra power, make the car very pleasant to drive. On a good, open stretch of road, speeds of about 80 m.p.h. were maintained for many miles, and the overdrive gives way to normal top at the touch of a switch. Overdrive middle gear was also useful, particularly in heavy traffic, making up largely for the slight decrease in the flexibility of the converted engine compared with the standard unit.

On the car tested the spring dampers at the rear were more firm than they are on the production Zephyr, which added to the handling qualities, and the brake linings were of an anti-fade type. The brakes did not fade during the test, but more than normal pedal pressure was required. Certainly the car did feel safe, to an almost surprising degree, at high speed.

Minimum m.p.g. recorded was 21. This was when the car was driven really hard, and the overdrive ratios used not as a means of lowering r.p.m. but as extra gears, there to be used to the full. This figure is about the same as the minimum for the standard car. With this high-efficiency engine conversion and overdrive, used more economically, it should be possible to achieve excellent m.p.g. The price of the conversion (excluding overdrive) is £100, plus £5 for fitting.

Six inlet ports are fed by the two inclined S.U. carburettors. The battery is moved to the luggage locker to make room for the manifolding and to improve the weight distribution.

Opal Blue was listed as an export colour, but occasionally appeared on a home market car. DRC 401 is a well-preserved original example of the early Consul.

The rear threequarter view of the same car emphasises the very clean styling of the smooth basic shape, a shape introduced at a time when large curved mudguards attached to somewhat narrower bodies, were still almost the norm.

"You can have any colour you like, so long as it's black,"
Henry Ford is supposed to have once said, and certainly,
despite the lovely new pastel shades available, many
people still favoured the more traditional black during the
early 1950s. This colour suited the new body shape, as
exemplified here on a very original 1953 Zephyr Six.

Some of the black-painted cars featured a
gunmetal-coloured facia.

Red upholstery and trim always looked well on the
black-painted cars. This Zephyr displays the standard
PVC seating which usually proved to be very
hard-wearing, and certainly easier to look after than
ageing leather.

The most subtle of the Zodiac's two-tone paint schemes is the Dorchester Grey (upper) and Bristol Fawn combination. Judging by the number of surviving Zodiacs in this scheme, it was the most popular, too.

Left. One of the rare black Zodiacs reveals its magnificent engine bay. The red-painted rocker cover and cylinder head were standard Zodiac items.

Below. Consuls, too, could be made to glow. Non-standard in its two-tone paint with metallic finish, this Consul nevertheless epitomises the 'fifties scene.

Right. The rather discreet bonnet motif of the late model Consul. Here detail of the grille and its badging can also be clearly seen.

Below. The full view reveals RRU 737 to be one of the rare Farnham estate cars, thought to be the only one in fact in regular use in Britain today. With optional overriders, the Consul is well endowed with 'fifties-style chrome plate.

The million-dollar look – British style.

Ivory was listed as an export-only colour, making this a very rare convertible in Britain.

Above. A safety-glass rear window is a rare fitting amongst drophead cars, which usually feature a celluloid or plastic rear window. The hood is in a heavy-duty PVC coated material.

Below. Facing the convertible driver was a similar layout to that of the saloons. Just visible here, beneath the parcel shelf on the extreme right, is the switch for the power-operated hood mechanism.

Right. Step in – for a sunshine ride. The ivory/white combination certainly conjures up dreams of sunnier climates than Britain's, but when the fog clears, or after the storms have passed, what better way to enjoy the British summer than in a Zephyr Six convertible?

The Grey/Blue Zodiac colour scheme is comparatively rare today, making this restored car a welcome sight indeed.

Genuine gold-plated script – on an £851 car!

OWNER'S VIEW

Michael Allen interviews Andy Tutt who has a Mk1 Consul amongst his small collection of cars which include an Anglia and an MGB. Andy recently took on the role of spares secretary in the Mk1 owners' club.

M.A. Why are you so interested in the Mk1 Fords?
A.T. I loved them as a child, I used to stare at them and wish my father would buy one, but actually he always bought Austins ...
M.A. When did you eventually buy your own Mk1?
A.T. I bought my Consul in August 1983, principally because it was in generally sound condition without needing any new panels or welding. I had started with a Zodiac which had proved to be too far gone to save, so this basically solid Consul seemed to be a much more attractive proposition.
M.A. Just what condition was the Consul in then?
A.T. Well, tatty looking, but actually very solid indeed. It had done 90,000 miles on the original engine which was well-worn.
M.A. So, what renovation have you carried out so far?
A.T. Bodily, some lead loading and a respray, all carried out professionally. Mechanically, an

engine rebuild which was also a professional job, and some work on the front suspension and brakes.
M.A. Was there any problem getting parts?
A.T. No, a local engineering firm did the engine overhaul, and they supplied the new pistons and shells, etc.
M.A. In view of this work would it have been more economic to have purchased a better example initially?
A.T. Possibly, although this one wasn't expensive to buy in the first place.
M.A. How you do rate the performance and handling of the Mk1 Consul in today's conditions?
A.T. The performance is adequate, in fact it rolls along quite fast if necessary. It handles well, and I certainly enjoy driving it, there are no problems at all as far as I'm concerned.
M.A. Is it in regular use now?
A.T. Not all the time, it has spells of everyday use though.
M.A. When needed regularly does it prove to be a practical proposition?
A.T. Very practical. As you know, I'm spares secretary for the Mk1 club, and I'm able to take many items to club meetings in the Consul with it being so roomy, and sometimes tow a trailer full of spares too. We have used it also this year to go on holiday to France.
M.A. Are the running costs high?
A.T. It averages about 26mpg, and spares prices are certainly cheaper than for modern cars, and cheaper than for my MGB.
M.A. Has your car won any prizes in concours or similar events?
A.T. No prizes yet, but it did get a ''commended'' at a local show.
M.A. How helpful do you think it is to be a member of the Mk1 owners' club?
A.T. Well, before I became a club officer I found it very helpful in respect of advice, etc, and now of course we are widening the club's scope with regard to spare parts.

M.A. Outside the club is there a spares specialist whom you have found particularly helpful?
A.T. Yes, John Blythe of Goldendays Motor Services. He supplied me with some suspension parts when I had the front suspension overhauled.
M.A. How would you sum up the enjoyment you get from the Consul?
A.T. I enjoy driving it, and taking it to shows and club meetings. I enjoy doing some work on it, and like to think that every time I show it it is marginally better than the previous time. Just carrying out small improvements yourself can give a lot of pleasure.
M.A. Finally, what advice would you give to potential Mk1 Consul owners?
A.T. Join the Mk1 club and enjoy the friendship of other similar minded people.

Michael Allen talks to Leeds businessman Steve Scott, owner of a 1955 Zephyr Zodiac, and a modern continental six-cylinder car for business use.

M.A. Why are you so interested in the Mk1 Fords?
S.S. I had one in the late 1960s, a Zephyr Six, when I was 18. They were in their ''banger'' days then of course, and I bought it for £25, but I thought it was a superb car. Out of all my early cars that was the one which made a terrific impression.
M.A. When and why did you buy your present Zodiac?
S.S. I saw a review of your book ''Consul Zephyr Zodiac'' and ordered a copy right away, after reading it I realised I just had to get another Mk1. That was 18 months ago.
M.A. What condition was the car in?
S.S. Basically sound, but a bit frayed around the edges, particularly the wings. The paint wasn't too good either, but the interior was very tidy which is always a good thing, and at a

genuine 64,000 miles there were no real problems mechanically.

M.A. What renovation has been done since?

S.S. I managed to locate new front wings and a front panel, and one rear wing. These have been fitted and the car resprayed after repairs to the other rear wing and rear valance. I've had some new chrome items, too.

M.A. What advice would you give to someone else facing similar work on the Mk1?

S.S. Ask around amongst other enthusiasts about a good garage, be very careful who you get to do bodywork repairs and painting.

M.A. Would it in fact have been more economic to have bought a better Mk1 in the first place?

S.S. Oh yes, but although there are some really superb Zodiacs around, they rarely come up for sale, so I picked the first sound one and put the necessary work in hand.

M.A. Have you experienced any difficulties in obtaining parts?

S.S. It took some time to locate the wings, but otherwise no problems. I've had some mechanical and service items more recently, and with the club, Newford Parts Centre, Ford 50 Spares, and Goldendays Motor Services you can usually get just what you want.

M.A. How do you rate the performance?

S.S. I find the performance exhilarating, the throttle response and mid-range power are superb, I enjoy driving it around just for that. To be honest, though, I wish it would stop as well as it can go.

M.A. And the handling qualities?

S.S. Very good, that is, once you get used to the fact that the cross-ply tyres don't have the grip of modern radials. Having got used to that it doesn't cause any problems, and in fact the car handles really well.

M.A. Is your Mk1 in regular use?

S.S. Yes, although not everyday. I use it for business much more than I intended simply because I

enjoy it so much.

M.A. Is it in fact practical for everyday use in today's conditions?

S.S. Very practical really, and it always gives the impression that it likes being worked hard, it's certainly not a fragile car.

M.A. Are the running costs high?

S.S. Oh no, very low in fact taken overall. I do run a modern up-market car as you know, and by comparison the Zodiac is cheaper to maintain and run by so much as to be out of all recognition. Of course, it was obviously designed with ease of maintenance in mind, which rarely seems to be the case with modern cars.

M.A. Has your Zodiac won any prizes in concours or similar events?

S.S. No, the standards now are very high, but I do intend my car to become competitive, and will be spending more on improving its condition further.

M.A. Do you enter it in any form of motorsport.

S.S. Yes, recently I entered a short road-rally organised by two old-established motor clubs in Yorkshire. The event took place in the Yorkshire Dales over a route of about 80 miles which was split into separately timed stages. As much of the route consisted of narrow twisting roads, and with plenty of hills, the compact Mk1 with its six-cylinder power proved very suitable and I finished 3rd in the postwar class of about 20 cars. I found this event very enjoyable, and would like to do more.

M.A. You obviously do enjoy the performance of the Mk1 Zodiac, so how much did you enjoy the recent motorway trip south to the big Mk1 meeting?

S.S. Superb, a lot of fun. Several Mk1s travelled down in loose convoy as you know, and that was great. Coming back on my own I

found the faster run very exhilarating, it surprised a lot of people on the motorway; it was foot to the floor a lot of the time actually, which is a bit noisy on a Mk1 without overdrive, but a nice thrill to be in the outside lane most of the time.

M.A. Did you check the fuel consumption on that run?

S.S. For the 360 mile round trip it was about 22mpg, I think it did about 20mpg coming home.

M.A. How helpful is it being a member of the owners' club?

S.S. I've found it very helpful indeed for advice about the Mk1 and running one today. It's also worth being in for the meetings and friendships.

M.A. Is there a specialist whom you have found to be particularly useful?

S.S. I have used them all, including buying spares from the club, it was very useful to be able to pay by credit card at the Newford Parts Centre.

M.A. How would you sum up the enjoyment you get from your Mk1 Zodiac?

S.S. The opportunity to drive regularly something that is basically of a better quality than the modern mass-produced Euro tin boxes.

M.A. What advice have you for potential owners of a Mk1 Zephyr or Zodiac?

S.S. Buy the best one you can afford, professional restoration work is expensive and a cheap car may require considerable work which will make it expensive by the time it's in the condition you really want. Join the Mk1 club of course, and drive your Mk1 regularly to get the full pleasure out of it, as they drive so well.

BUYING

Which model?

Whilst in no way a fast car today, but nevertheless capable of exceeding 70mph, and pulling smoothly from as little as 20mph in top gear in a manner out of all recognition by comparison with today's four-cylinder cars, the Consul can offer entirely adequate performance with which to cope with modern conditions. A touring fuel consumption in the 30mpg region should be easily obtainable, and the 1.5-litre engine is advantageous in that it attracts only low insurance premiums. Many of the features which made the Consul so popular 30 years ago are still quite valid today. Good headroom, and easy access are typical of the commonsense this model displayed throughout; and these features, combined with what are usually perfectly reasonable asking prices for this model today, all indicate a thoroughly usable and economical way of "classic" motoring.

Offering the same accommodation, but with rather better appointments, the Zephyr differs principally of course by virtue of its six-cylinder engine of 50% greater displacement. On the road, this adds up to top gear acceleration around 50% faster between 20 and 40mph, whilst above about 50mph the Zephyr accelerates twice as quickly as the four-cylinder car and attains a usefully higher maximum speed. The price for all this is an overall fuel consumption worse by about 5mpg, although of course if the extra performance is not habitually used then the six-cylinder model can be quite economical for its engine size. Insurance premiums too are higher than for the Consul, as are usually the prices asked. In most respects these comments apply equally to the Zodiac, although the additional glamour of this model almost always results in higher prices for what is generally regarded as the most "collectible" of the three models.

The choice then, to a large degree depends upon the desirability of the performance offered by the six-cylinder cars, plus of course the Zodiac's additional equipment and top-of-the-range status, or the excellent overall economy potential of the equally roomy Consul.

Examination

The simple, straightforward mechanical layout of these cars resulted in an excellent reputation for longevity, but a relatively low mileage example now could well be suffering the adverse effects of long periods out of use, and could be in need of some unexpected mechanical attention. Therefore, irrespective of the mileage covered, the car should be most thoroughly checked over as if it was a high mileage hardworked example.

Some fuming from the rocker cover breather/oil filler cap will be evident even from a really good engine, but if this is excessive and accompanied by a distinct "chuffing", and what appears to be similar to a misfire, then anticipate an engine overhaul being necessary. If the engine sounds well, and feels good on the road but nevertheless leaves a trail of blue smoke, then suspect the diaphragm on the vacuum pump as having split. If this is so, oil is sucked into the pump, thence the inlet manifold. In some cases, oiling up of plugs number 1 and 2, which are adjacent to the vacuum pipe connection at the manifold, is confirmation of this. Blue smoke momentarily when restarting a hot engine can usually be ignored, as this is due to no more than slight seepage past the valve stem oil seals, and which is rarely sufficient to have a significant effect on the overall oil consumption which is usually slight on a good example of these engines.

Expect some judder from the clutch, particularly when manoeuvring a fully warmed up car at speeds low enough to require slipping the clutch. Familiarity can largely overcome this problem however. A characteristic subdued whine may be heard when pulling away in the lower gears, top gear however should be silent. Second gear may jump out of engagement on the overrun with a well-worn gearbox, but this is a fault which can usually be attended to when convenient rather than being considered a matter of any urgency. If the synchromesh is in good condition, and the clutch is clearing properly, then gearchanging from first to second, and between second and top gear either way should be a pleasure, light, accurate and quick if necessary, this particular column change being widely regarded as the best of its type. Changing down into first gear on the move does require the double de-clutching technique. A subdued whine from the rear axle may be evident, but should certainly not be obtrusive. Incorrect pinion bearing pre-load can cause quite considerable "singing" from these axles, which adjustment can sometimes cure.

A good, but firm ride will be provided if the suspension is in good condition, any ''float'' over gentle undulations can be taken as indicating replacement of the front suspension units and rear dampers as being imminent. Expect the brakes to need firm pedal pressures even for normal retardation, and considerable effort from high speeds. Reasonably light at crawling speeds, the steering should feel pleasantly light and accurate on the road. The steering box is adjustable for wear, and is generally a long lasting item. Wear in any of the steering joints sufficient to cause any free play at the steering wheel rim will necessitate replacement joints. The availability of mechanical items for the Mk1 range from several sources means that all repairs are possible on these cars, and even if carried out professionally, the overall simplicity and excellent accessibility should keep labour costs down to a much more sensible level than is the case with similar types of modern car.

Thanks to a lot of work by the Mk1 owners' club in 1984, a variety of bodywork repair sections for this model's vulnerable areas are now available to club members, thus easing considerably many of the problems associated with restoring bodywork. When inspecting a Mk1, it is as well to remember that the extensive corrosion which can effect the entire trailing edge of the front wings may have spread to the adjacent area of the bulkhead to which the wing is bolted at this point. A similar situation may also be evident behind the leading vertical edge of the lower rear wing too, if this panel shows signs of coming adrift at its forward mounting point. The inner sills play an important part in the overall structural rigidity, as do the centre pillars, or B posts, and it is important that the B post attachment to the sill area is in

good condition: serious corrosion here is rare, but not entirely unknown. Otherwise, the usual common-sense checks should of course be made, and bearing in mind the present good spares situation a purchase can be made if the price reflects the condition. It is hardly worth bothering attempting a total restoration on a really rotten hulk of a Mk 1 saloon as, relatively speaking, there are quite a number of basically good ones around.

In respect of the extremely rare convertibles, a different view sometimes has to be taken, as first class examples can be considered as almost never coming up for sale. Apart from the obvious checks here, it is essential to remember that the additional X-bracing welded into the floorpan must be in perfect condition if the convertible is not to display quite noticeable shake on the road. Repair sections here will have to be fabricated on a one-off basis.

Historical value patterns

At a time when new car shortages were pushing used car prices up to higher levels than similar new models, government action came in the form of a two year covenant (precluding the resale of the vehicle within that period) which every new car buyer had to sign on taking delivery. In force at the time of the Mk1's introduction, this restriction did not last long into the 1950s, although waiting lists for these cars resulted in relatively high prices being asked for used examples throughout their production run. Obsolescence in 1956 caused only a slight drop in value, and in fact the widespread popularity of this range was such

that it was not until after 1960 that cheap, but still sound examples were to be found in significant numbers. Their ''banger'' days quickly followed, during which, according to condition rather than model, they were either cheap, or very cheap indeed.

In recent years, since being recognised as genuine postwar classics, prices have tended to follow the original new car pattern, in that for any given condition the Zephyrs are more expensive than Consuls, with the Zodiacs demanding higher prices still. Overall, however, their present day values based on the actual amount of money which usually changes hands for a really good all-round Consul, Zephyr or Zodiac almost always represents excellent value by comparison with similarly priced modern cars which are heading quickly towards their demise at the bottom of the used car market.

Summing up

Any Mk1 which is in a sound condition, and running in a manner similar to that which Dagenham intended, is a perfectly practical proposition for regular use today. Prices within the collectors' car scene are usually sensible enough, and restoration is now actually easier than it was some years ago as Mk1 club members have access to a good range of bodywork repair sections. Nevertheless, as with any collectors' car, it does usually pay to purchase the best available rather than undertake an extensive restoration to high standards.

CLUBS, SPECIALISTS & BOOKS

Clubs

The tangible benefits gained by joining the appropriate owners' club vary somewhat depending upon just what services the particular club offers its members. In the case of the Mk1 Owners' Club in Britain, these services are a regular newsletter with quite varied content and at least three major national meetings a year, including a road-run, as well as club participation in many "open" events. The club has a spare parts policy which aims to supplement the parts availability from the various specialists in respect of routine-service and mechanical items, whilst also offering a range of remanufactured bodywork repair panels available exclusively through the club. Being a national club, with its 300 plus members being spread rather widely throughout Britain, there is naturally less emphasis placed on the social side than on help and advice with both technical and other matters over which a non-member might have difficulty.

Several clubs catering for these models also exist in Australia and New Zealand, but on a rather more local basis due to the vast distances between townships in Australia particularly. Due to the relative scarcity of these cars "down under", the clubs there generally encompass all models, Marks 1 to 4, of the long running Consul Zephyr Zodiac series.

Five Stars – Mk1 Consul Zephyr Zodiac Owners' Club
Neil Tee, Membership Secretary, 8 Park Farm Close, Shadoxhurst, Nr. Ashford, Kent TN26 1LD, England.

Five Stars – Mk1 Consul Zephyr Zodiac Owners' Club (New Zealand)
Grant Lousich, 20 Sawyers Arms Road, Papanui, Christchurch 5, New Zealand.

Consul Zephyr Zodiac Club (Wellington Inc.)
Bob Crozier, PO Box 1585, Wellington, New Zealand.

Auckland Consul Zephyr Zodiac Car Club
Graeme Parsons, PO Box 30179, Takapuna North, Auckland, New Zealand.

The Zodiac and Zephyr Club (Southland) Inc.
5 Nevis Crescent, Invercargill, New Zealand.

Zephyr Zodiac Car Club (Christchurch) Inc.
Mrs. Maureen Anthony, PO Box 21157, Christchurch, New Zealand.

Zephyr Zodiac Club of Otago
Peter Matheson, 16 Eglington Road, Dunedin, New Zealand.

Nelson Zephyr Zodiac Club
Tim Readley, 10 Colman Street, Richmond, Nelson, New Zealand.

Classic Zephyr Zodiac Enthusiasts Club
Greg Price, c/o The Post Office, Paremoremo, Auckland, New Zealand.

Zephyr Zodiac Club (Herewhenua)
John Clime, 10 Margret Street, Levin, New Zealand.

Zephyr Zodiac Owners' Club (Central Region)
Bryan Brickley, PO Box 5128, Palmerston North, New Zealand.

Hamilton Zephyr Zodiac Club
Mrs Rochelle Hooper, PO Box 4295, Hamilton East, New Zealand.

Consul Zephyr Zodiac Club of New South Wales
John Bourke, 172 Ridge Road, Engadine, NSW, Australia.

Zephyr and Zodiac Owners' Club of Melbourne
PO Box 86, Surrey Hills, Victoria, Australia.

Consul Zephyr Zodiac Car Club of Queensland
PO Box 279, Salisbury 4107, Queensland, Australia.

Zephyr Zodiac Owners' Club of Western Australia
Mrs. Sue Roberts, 70a Glenelg Avenue, Wembley Downs, Western Australia.

Spares specialists

Some service items can still be obtained occasionally at motor factors, and, on more of a pot luck basis, valuable items can still be found on the stalls at autojumbles. Much of what is needed however will almost certainly have to come from one of the specialists dealing with the models in question, particularly so in respect of reconditioned exchange items.

Goldendays Motor Services (Prop. J. Blythe)
Boundary Garage, Cromer Road, Norwich, England.

Ford 50 Spares (Prop. K. Tingey)
69 Jolliffe Road, Poole, Dorset BH15 2HA, England.

Newford Parts Centre (Prop. J. Horridge)
Abbey Mill, Abbey Village, Chorley, Lancashire, England.

Books

Several of the owners' handbook type, and the rather more comprehensive repair manuals were published during the 1950s and 1960s for these cars. All, bar one, however, are now out of print, but do nevertheless turn up occasionally on the shelves of specialist motoring book shops, and of course on autojumble stalls.

The Ford Motor Company's own workshop manuals and spare parts manuals were originally distributed throughout the Ford dealership network primarily for their own use, however examples of these extremely useful books can be found today on the secondhand car book market.

Still in print and available is the "**Ford Consul Zephyr and Zodiac MkI, II & III Owner's Workshop Manual.**" Published by the Haynes Publishing Group, this manual deals comprehensively with maintenance and all major repair procedures on the Mk1 and subsequent Mk2 and Mk3 models

From the historical point of view, nothing was published about these cars until my own major work on the subject: "**Consul Zephyr Zodiac: The Big Fifties Fords,**" appeared in

November 1983. This is an in-depth history, including full competition history, of both the Mk1 and the Mk2 range. Published by Motor Racing Publications, it is still in print and widely available.

PHOTO GALLERY

1

1. The Consul and Zephyr Six as introduced. The additional embellishments of the six-cylinder models such as the plated screen surround inserts and side window surrounds, wing flashes, bonnet motif, and overriders are all evident. The Zephyr depicted was one of the press demonstrators, and was road-tested by "The Motor".

2. The winged badge of the Zephyr Six was repeated on the boot lid, and was only a feature of the early flat-dashboard models. A wingless version of this badge appeared at the front only on the Consul.

3. Zephyr Six interior. The pushbutton radio was an optional extra. A replica of the front and rear badge adorns the glovebox lid, and the doorpull/armrest which were a Zephyr only feature can just be seen. The elegant horn ring sounds a powerful twin horn installation.

4. No badge, and no horn ring identify this as the Consul facia. A blanking cover is in position over the aperture for the radio, and swivelling ashtrays are situated at each end.

2

3

4

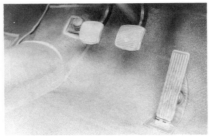

5. In addition to the speedometer are a fuel gauge and ammeter. In some export markets an engine temperature gauge – in place of the ammeter – could be specified. Behind what appear to be two screws, are in fact the oil pressure warning light (left) and the ignition warning light.

6. The accelerator pedal on the early cars did not conform to the new pendant arrangements for the clutch and brakes. The headlamp dipswitch can be seen alongside the clutch pedal. Lifting the floor covering away from the transmission tunnel reveals a removable plate giving access to the gearbox oil-level dipstick.

7. A line up of engine/gearbox units destined for installation in left-hand-drive cars. The oil bath air cleaner was a standard export fitting, although in this case it is unlikely that these engines are going to hot, dusty climates, as the standard two-bladed fans are fitted; four-bladed fans were usually fitted on cars sent

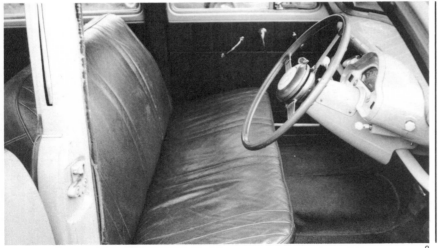

to hot countries. The gearbox dipstick can be clearly seen, as can the handbrake cables and linkage already attached to the gearbox rear-support member.

8 & 9. Interior views of a late 1952 Consul showing the curved dash panel introduced into production in September that year. A pull-out ashtray was situated centrally in the new dash panel. The swivelling ashtray provided for rear seat passengers can be seen in the back of the front seat squab. The chrome doorpulls were optional extras.

10, 11 & 12. Curved-dash models can be identified externally by a larger grille badge, and, at the rear, by the fact that the chrome strip running the length of the car at shoulder height terminates along the top of the rear wing, having previously continued down to the boot opening level. The bonnet motif on DRC 401 is a non-Ford accessory item.

13

14

15

17

18

16

19

13. The new grille badge in position on the Zephyr Six post September 1952.

14. Close up detail of the revised badge fitted from September 1952. "A Ford Product. Made in England": there were no formal links between Dagenham and Cologne in those days ...

15 & 16. The name scripts were chrome-plated castings, and remained unaltered in style throughout the production run. The front bumpers on the early cars were not interchangeable, that on the Zephyr Six having a constant curvature whereas the Consul's had an almost flat centre section.

17 & 18. The rear-end treatment differed far less between the two models than at the front. The bumpers here are interchangeable, but the badge, chromed numberplate-lamp cover and overriders distinguish the six-cylinder car. Both cars here depict the original tail/stoplight combined units. The reflectors on the Consul are genuine Ford accessories, whereas those fitted on the Zephyr's back panel are non-Ford items, as are the flashing indicators alongside which have been fitted retrospectively to this 1953 semaphore equipped car.

19. A roomy luggage compartment was provided, with access to the spare wheel being easy, although the high back panel does impede loading and unloading somewhat. The 9 gallon fuel tank resides externally beneath the boot, its filler cap just to the right of the number plate. At the top of the picture, the number plate lamps can be seen illuminated.

20, 21, 22, 23. More close up details of the pre-October 1953 cars. The Consul's plain rubber screen surround; the Zephyr-only bonnet motif and front wing ornament; and the semaphore indicators common to both models.

24. The optional push-button radio designed for the curved-dash cars. The engine temperature and oil pressure gauges are non-Ford accessories. The heating and demisting controls can be seen beneath the shelf, as can be the pistol-grip handbrake lever.

25. The speaker was mounted just above the windscreen. This view shows the cloth roof lining and the sunvisors which, although not readily apparent here, are covered in the same material.

26. The large oil-bath air cleaner dominates the under bonnet view of this export Consul which saw service in the West Indies before returning to England. An oil-bath rocker cover breather/oil filler cap is also fitted as was often the case with cars destined for hot, dry climates.

27. Another interesting Consul underbonnet scene, this time showing a twin SU carburettor conversion. Several such conversions were available from tuning specialists, as were triple carburettor installations for the six-cylinder cars.

28. The two diagonal members which transfer some of the suspension loads into the bulkhead structure can be seen in this view of the six-cylinder engine compartment. The common reservoir (with internal division) for the brake and clutch master cylinders is at the top left, with the bulkhead-mounted cylinders themselves just being hidden from view. The Smith's heater unit and its blower occupy much of the offside space. When leaving Dagenham, the rocker cover and air cleaner were painted black on both Consuls and Zephyrs, unlike the chrome-plated fittings on this otherwise standard underbonnet scene.

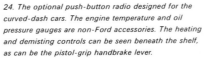

30

31

32

33

29. The chassis plate is mounted on the nearside of the engine compartment front bulkhead. The engine number here indicates a late model six-cylinder car.

30, 31, 32. The magnificent Zephyr Zodiac introduced the deeper bumpers and full length chrome side strips to the entire range.

33. The two-tone paint division gave a rather longer look to the Zephyr Zodiac.
Black Zodiacs were available to special order.

34 & 35. The new front wing ornament incorporated the ''Five Star'' theme. The lockable fuel filler cap and reversing lamp are standard Zodiac equipment. The separate indicator light in the back panel denotes a post October 1955 car.

34

35

36

37

38

39

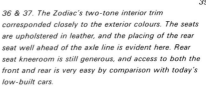

40

36 & 37. The Zodiac's two-tone interior trim corresponded closely to the exterior colours. The seats are upholstered in leather, and the placing of the rear seat well ahead of the axle line is evident here. Rear seat kneeroom is still generous, and access to both the front and rear is very easy by comparison with today's low-built cars.

38 & 39. The door trim styling was of a follow-through pattern. The lower sections are finished in carpeting to match the sills and floor.

40. The Zodiac facia and steering wheel were as on the Zephyr Six. The previous push-button radio was at first optional equipment on the Zodiac before being superseded by the type shown here with drum tuning on which a hinged flap opens to reveal the drums. When factory fitted, this radio came with twin speakers, one in the nearside of the front parcel shelf and one centrally in the rear compartment shelf. The T handles beneath the shelf on the right are the bonnet release (left) and the overdrive manual lock-out control.

41, 42, 43. The vanity mirror and electric clock were exclusive Zodiac features, but the interior light was shared with the cheaper cars.

41

42

43

44

45

46

48

47

50

49

52

51

53

44, 45, 46. The restyled and additional chrome embellishments, except the wheeltrim rings, appeared on the Zephyr Six at the same time the Zodiac was announced. This restored Zephyr Six displays a metal sunvisor and swivelling spotlamp, both of which were popular accessories in the 1950s. Whitewall tyres are also typical of the period.

47. The aeroplane-styled bonnet motif of the Zodiac and late model Zephyr Sixes.

48. Zephyr Six interior trim was to the same style now as the Zephyr Zodiac, but still in single colours, and with PVC seating. Single-tone leather seats were an optional extra, and on the Consul.

49. Front wheel and tyre detail of the Zephyr Six. The Consul rims were 0.5 inch narrower and with less offset than those on the six-cylinder cars. The jacking point socket is lost in shadow in this view, but is situated just ahead of the front door line.

50. Rear wheel and jacking point detail. The jack shown has a circular, universally-jointed base plate. Later jacks with similar to-and-fro operation had a triangular frame which resulted in a wider, more stable base. Zodiac jacks had an integral handle requiring a more convenient continuous circular motion to raise and lower the car.

51. The restyled bumpers were standardized on the Consul too, which now also featured the chrome inserts in the front and rear screen rubbers, and its own bonnet motif.

52. The Consul's shorter front wing with its different styling line necessitated a shorter "Five Star" wing flash.

53. Restyled Consul doortrim of October 1953 onwards. The check-stay which held the door in the open position is visible above the lower hinge. Just visible inside the car is the spoon-type accelerator with the short pedal pad.

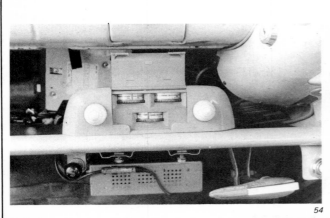

54

55

54. The later tuning-drum radio for the Consul and Zephyr Six models seen here with the flap open to reveal the tuning drums. As this Consul is devoid of a heater, the radio power-pack which is usually hidden from sight behind the heater controls can be seen quite clearly beneath the parcel shelf.

55. The radio aerial position recommended by Ford was chosen to allow the aerial, which was telescopic, to be raised or lowered without the driver having to leave the car.

56 & 57. Its two door arrangement, lower roof line (when the hood is in the raised position) and slightly higher side window base line combine to alter the proportions of the convertible quite noticeably by comparison with the saloons.

58. On the Zephyr Six convertible, shown here with the hood in the De Ville position, the hood is power operated by an electro/hydraulic system which also tilts the rear seat forward slightly during operation to avoid the hood interfering with the passenger's heads. The forward section can be arranged with the folds out of sight, and be secured in this position.

59. Extremely wide doors, in company with a split front seat squab which could be tipped forward, allowed reasonably good access to the rear compartment.

60. The stowage space required for the sidescreens reduced the width of the rear seat to two-seater proportions. No sunvisors were provided.

56

57

58

59

60

61

62

63

64

61. The Abbott estate car conversion utilised as much of the existing saloon as possible, retaining the saloon rear doors in their original form, and incorporating the original rear screen in the new tailgate. On the roof, rubber covered slats, strap eyes, and built in rails provided valuable extra stowage space.

62. The high rear panel was also retained, as was the normal boot floor and spare wheel well. This view shows the rear wing top chrome strip extending down to the rear lamp level: a feature reintroduced on the estate cars. This late model Consul displays the final tail lamp surround which included a separate reflector, and is one of the few Mk1s which has retained its original non-lockable fuel filler cap.

63. The extended roof line, and large additional side window give the false impression of a longer rear end as a whole, particularly so on the relatively short-nosed Consul.

64. A dashboard mounted rear-view mirror can be angled upwards for when the estate car is in a well-laden attitude. The late model long pedal pad accelerator is shown here.

65 & 66. Many export cars have survived and are still giving good service. These two views depict a much-decorated Consul which was photographed in Malta in the summer of 1985.

65

66

67

68

67. In sharp contrast, a remarkably original Maltese Zephyr Six photographed at the same time as the Consul depicted.

68. The Mk1 Zephyr's most famous competition success was outright victory in the Monte Carlo Rally of 1953: the winning car, VHK 194, and its driver Maurice Gatsonides being much photographed. Here, however, we see one of the other "works" Zephyrs heading for Monte Carlo that year, this being the car driven to 12th place overall by well known trials driver and Ford Main Dealer, TC. "Cuth" Harrison.

69. Sidney Allard's Zephyr at the end of the 1955 RAC Rally in which it finished 2nd in the up-to-2600cc GT category, just behind "Cuth" Harrison's similar car and ahead of the Reece cousin's Zephyr in 3rd place. The damage resulted from hitting a wall in Wales, and then a bridge parapet in the Lake District! The lack of a crumple-zone has preserved the car's geometry.

70. Hurrying through the night, Vic Preston pushes his Zephyr hard towards outright victory in the tough East African Safari Rally in 1955. Additional spotlamps are mounted high up near the screen to reduce the risk of damage from flying stones.

71. Another one of the three Zephyrs which finished the Safari in 1955. Matt black paint has been applied to this car in order to reduce dazzle from the African sunshine.

69

71

70